# Turn your setbacks into MAJOR COME-BACKS

**BASED ON A TRUE STORY**

*How to propel yourself to greatness using your setbacks*

## LAWRENCE A. NAMALE

MOTIVATING SPEAKER & LIFE COACH

**Turning Your Setbacks Into Major Comebacks**
© Copyright 2013 by Lawrence Akali Namale

All rights reserved. No part of this book may be used or reproduced in any manner whatsoever without written permission from Lawrence Namale, except as provided by the United States of America copyright law or in the case of brief quotations embodied in articles and reviews.

The scanning, uploading and distribution of this book via the Internet or via any other means without the permission of the publisher is illegal and punishable by law. Please purchase only authorized electronic editions and do not participate in or encourage electronic piracy of copyrighted materials. Your support of the author's rights is sincerely appreciated.

http://life-signatures.com

**Cover design and layout by:** MediaGraphics Studio
**Phone:** 0708-625252
**Email:** desgichuru@gmail.com

NOTE TO READERS
This publication contains the opinions and ideas of its author. It is intended to provide helpful and informative material on the subjects addressed. The strategies outlined in this book may not be suitable for every individual, and are not guaranteed or warranted to produce any particular results. This book is distributed (through sales or free gift) with the understanding that the author is not engaged in rendering legal, financial, accounting, or other professional advice or services. The reader should consult a competent professional before adopting any of the suggestions in this book or drawing inferences from it.

No warranty is made with respect to the accuracy or completeness of the information or references contained herein, and the author specifically disclaims any responsibility for any liability, loss or risk, personal or otherwise, which is incurred as a consequence, directly or indirectly, of the use and application of any of the contents of this book.

ISBN: 978-1508520412

# Dedication

*To Beth, my lover, friend and companion. You have come through and are a light to many. May your comebacks be complete in the fullness of time.*

*Dedication* ............................................................................................................. *iii*
*Endorsements* ....................................................................................................... *vii*
*Introduction* ............................................................................................................ 9

**CHAPTER 1: IT'S ALL COMMON TO MAN**
One of man's greatest occupation is to create a life totally devoid of heartache, hardship, and setbacks. It could be like chasing a mirage trying to live a life without experiencing any crisis of sorts especially in this 'fallen world.' Should we embrace trouble or should we seek to experience life outside of it? ............................................................. 13

**CHAPTER 2: WHAT CAUSES PEOPLE TO GET STUCK?**
The need to understand that a Life Crisis can either be created by our actions, whether good or bad, or by circumstances and situations beyond our control. Either way, our staying stuck in either case is as a result of our choices .............. 41

**CHAPTER 3: "UNLESS THOSE DAYS ARE SHORTENED…"**
Who does not want to spend the least number of days in a crisis? Who does not want to know the answers to the deepest questions of their lives at the shortest possible time? Who does not want the duration of a heartache to be shorter? ............................................................................................................... 61

**CHAPTER 4: THE DARK SIDE OF HOPE**
The greatest paradox in a crisis is hoping for the light to come at the end of the tunnel, trusting the Divine to help us against taking matters into our own hands. Hope is good, hoping is critical, but there is a dark side of it ..................... 85

**CHAPTER 5: THE BEAUTY OF ADVERSITY**
It is always a wonder that countless people from all over the world are most grateful after an adversity, not that it is over, but that it has made them better. They are deeper, wiser, stronger, and more spiritual ............................ 105

**CHAPTER 6: THE FOLLY AND LESSONS IN TAKING SHORTCUTS**
We are most vulnerable to glittering bait when we are in a crisi because. we want it to end as quickly as possible. Most importantly we blindly hope to come out of it without any side effects. But do shortcuts help? .................... 123

**CHAPTER 7: THE ABUNDANCE OF OPTIONS**
A great illusion created by an adversity is that we are stuck and there is nothing we can do apart from either waiting for God to help us, or for time to bring respite. Do we have anything we can do about a crisis to ignite an immediate change? ............................................................................................................... 141

**CHAPTER 8: THE BIGGEST SECRET IN GOD'S CREATION: WHERE ARE YOU NOW?**
God has one major secret in all of His creation. It applies to all living things as well as all the elements of nature He created. That secret also applies to man but cannot be seen with the 'naked eye' ................................................. 157

**CHAPTER 9: 21 WAYS TO COME OUT BETTER: NUGGETS TO NAVIGATE A CRISIS**
A revolution is within reach, certainly during a crisis. Simple and practical steps applied while the crisis lasts will ignite a fundamental change that will last a life time ............................................................................................... 179

**CHAPTER 10: THERE IS HOPE!**
As much as adversity is common to man, there is always hope with each setback faced. Many people come out of it and so will you ............................................................................................................... 211

**CHAPTER 11: EPILOGUE**

# Endorsements

"The book looks like it's going to be a must have, quite well laid out and the information is so timely in this day and age as we really need to dust ourselves off many a time and get back on the saddle"
-**Phillip Kambe, Founder and Executive Coach, Intelligent Performance International**

"Very often the things we call setbacks, resistances and failures make positive contribution to our success as well. The chick would not get fully developed without the resistance of the egg shell during hatching; eagles would be unable to soar without air resistance; mistakes are transformed from liabilities into assets when you learn from them. Lawrence Namale, beautifully shows why and how you can turn your setbacks into major comebacks!"
-**James Abola: Author, Business Consultant and Money Management Coach.**

"I have enjoyed Lawrence's style of writing, how he's derived profound lessons from life experiences. It's not often that people ponder on life's challenges and victories while asking themselves how Point A brought them to Point B and how the lessons gathered can influence their journey to Point C. *Turn Your Setbacks to Major Comebacks* has done just that, challenging the reader to go beyond the surface and take personal responsibility for their success and growth. I recommend this book to every person who is serious about overcoming obstacles and finding success in life, career and business"
-**Ngina Otiende, Marriage Mentor and Author of** *"Blues to Bliss: Creating Happily Ever After In the Early Years"*

"In this captivating, practical, and easy read treatise, Lawrence not only showcases some great literary prowess but goes on to help you turn adversity into advancement. If you want to turn your setbacks into setups to greatness look no further".
**Anthony T. Gitonga, International Leadership Speaker & Author of** *"Made for Greatness."*

"I have read many books but none is as easy as this one. The author brings out the power packaged messages with a beautiful story of Ben, to show indeed that we can Turn our Setbacks into Major Comebacks. I like the fact that he invites our minds to think right and ask relevant questions in regard to our destinies.

One of the greatest revelations that I can resonate within my life is flipping a question of "Why me" to other objective questions of "Who am I and Where am I going". Namale has addressed everyday issues in a very well thought manner that provokes your thinking to move from just a pity party of setbacks to major life comebacks.

This book is a must read for people who are seeking to breakthrough into the mindset of greatness. I am sure it will revolutionize your thinking just as it did to me."

**Wambui Njuguna, Author of** *"Picking up the Pieces"*

# *Introduction*

> *"The most beautiful people I've known are those who have known trials, have known struggles, have known loss and have found their way out of the depths."*
>
> -Elisabeth Kübler-Ross

In 2012, America was on the brink of another major milestone. Having elected Barrack Obama, as President in 2008, the next hurdle in history would be his re-election. As it is customary in the American democracy, Presidential candidates take on each other in public debates over issues affecting their nation and what they and their respective governments would do.

In the first debate with Governor Mitt Romney, it is widely recorded that Barrack Obama performed dismally. He seemed like a boxer in the ring with his hands hanging down, allowing his opponent lots of room to throw in one devastating jab after another. Obama seemed a pale shadow of himself, so docile that his entire following got worried.

That was a major 'setback' in the Obama re-election campaign. Yet I would say that that was one of the sweetest things that ever happened. Till today, looking at the eventual comeback, you would excuse me for thinking that that dismal performance was stage-managed. We all know Obama to be much better than what he exuded in the first debate.

However, in the successive debates, Barrack Obama mounted one of the greatest come-backs I have seen in modern history. He was thorough. He was smart. He taunted the Governor. He interrupted him. The sweetest part of that showdown was when Governor Romney made a mistake to claim that it took more than a week or so for President Obama to label the attack on the American embassy in Benghazi as an act of terror. Obama feasted on that error by Romney to crown his immaculate performance that day.

In retrospect, you could say the setback in Obama's campaign was a good thing. It simply was a setup, or better, a stepping stone into being re-elected. It was one of the key *catalysts* in the 2012 American Presidential elections.

This book is about comebacks, and how we can orchestrate our own revivals.

Everyone is entitled to his or her comeback in life. Over the course of our existence, we face a setback or a crisis or some form of hardship. The wise thing to do would be to know how best we can leverage the hold up and mount a major return. This book purposes to deal with this comprehensively. Naturally when a crisis hits us, we label it as a negative. We want to deal with it immediately so that our lives can revert back to the 'normal' that we are used to.

The truth of the matter is that after a crisis, you might not know 'normal' as you used to, and neither should you. After the crisis, depending on how you handled it, you will either be grateful that it did happen but never want to go through it again, or you will lay blame on the crisis for your misfortune for the next few years to come.

I believe that the former is much more common, and this book is full of nuggets that will most definitely help you through the *four phases* of the crisis life cycle. Like Obama, you will learn that in retrospect the setback can be used as a setup for a major comeback.

There is a beautiful purpose in all the setbacks we will face, and this purpose cannot be de-linked from the very essence of life. Throughout the *four phases* of a life crisis, there is one major anchor that holds it up together.

All humans must face adversity at one point in life, and how we handle each is significant. Any attempt to try living in a world devoid of hardship and setbacks is defeatist. If you face the setbacks head-on with the knowledge that it is temporary, will be set up to coming out better and with a higher *resilience index*.

While on a working assignment in Ghana, I met a young, bubbly and exuberant lady who was an executive in one of the leading corporate organizations in the country. Over the course of our interactions, it turned out that this girl was separated from her philandering husband. When she mentioned her marital setback in passing, I honestly thought she was kidding. It turned out that she was serious.

I was amazed with the ease at which she volunteered the information. It was almost as if she and resigned to her fate. It seemed she belonged to a school of thought that says, "This is the 21$^{st}$ century and these things happen". Sarah was not married for more than a year before trouble showed up in her marriage. Her ex-husband was non-committal, but thoroughly inconsistent in taking care of their child.

Sarah is beautiful, no doubt and extremely talented, intelligent and resourceful. A single conversation with her revealed that she was smart, had a healthy sense of humor and a good world view. But Sarah was experiencing one of the major setbacks of her life. Her dad had passed on earlier while she was a young girl of 5 years. The grim prospect of her daughter spending the rest of her life without a father figure was real…yet Sarah seemed resigned to fate.

Her bubbly character and always available and hearty laughter betrayed what was going on in her life. Her speech told me that she was scared of loving someone else again. That was her ultimate fear. The good thing with Sarah is that she has the most teachable attitude that I have ever seen in many people.

I started speaking to her and applying some of the principles that I am sharing in this book. I coached her for over three months on a weekly basis. First of all, we got rid of her speech that was all doom and gloom of the past and existing setback. We got her to love herself. Over and over again, we got her to understand that she deserves a better and joyous life.

Most importantly, we got Sarah to start dreaming and making little adjustments in her life. She had a pending divorce that was not settled because she was vacillating over it. Her ex-husband was already living with someone else, sure grounds for divorce in scripture. We got her to start 'cleaning house' and deal with all the clutter of her life.

I told Sarah that if she wanted the new (which she had now come to accept as a major possibility), she would need to get rid of the old, both psychologically and physically. Within those three months, Sarah's possibilities began to unfold. Someone who had been her friend for years all of a sudden grew interested in her. While there can be no guarantee that this new relationship will work (actually people need to work on relationships instead of waiting for it to work), one thing is for sure: One soul was stuck and had generally accepted a setback as her fate, but now the 'lights have come on' and she can now explore her possibilities that will always be boundless.

This book is for people such as Sarah who are living with setbacks as if there are no options for comebacks.

Contrary to common belief, there are loads of valuable things that you can do, adjustments that you can make in a crisis that will make you better and wiser by the time you come through it. My prophecy is this: You will come through the setback. However, using this crisis to your advantage is the chief purpose for writing this book.

A very common strategy that people employ during a crisis is to 'wait'. Some people resort to prayers (which have their place) and waiting for God to come through for them. If/when God does not show up, it leaves them disillusioned. You will learn through this book that there are things that you can do 'while waiting'. There is a controversial chapter in the book titled "The Dark Side of Hope" that is a must read especially for those who heavily rely on divine intervention.

Obviously, adversities, hardships and setbacks are not comfortable things to handle. They are difficult. The world is cruel that sometimes a common feedback we get is "Get over it!" To the unprepared, that is one of the harsh statements you will hear. In essence, 'get over it' is the stark reminder that there is nothing you can do, and that you should shape up or ship out.

However, at some instances, that statement is laden with nothing but truth. If this truth is accepted early, one can deal with it. One can easily get better equipped with handling the repercussions of that truth and move on. A truth on trial in life is this: 'Life Is Not fair'. So what do you do with that statement? We'll find out later on in the book.

This book incorporates events based on the true life story of a young executive who gets stuck in his career, lost his job and got evicted from his rental house. Ben, our character, thought that everything was going well for him until a setback hit him hard.

Through his story, we will learn things that Ben did as well as those he should have done now that he looks back at his crisis in retrospect.

Corresponding to the 21 ways that a crisis makes you a better person, there is a bonus of 21 things that you should *not do* while in a crisis. You can download the E-book worth $10 from http://life-signatures.com for free. From the same website, you will also have access to a 'Crisis Management Work Book' that includes exercises that you can use with every one of the 21 concepts discussed in this book.

It is my belief that through this book, your understanding of the cycle of crises will help you change your perspective about your setbacks and help you mount major comebacks every time you face an adversity in most, if not all areas of your life.

# CHAPTER 1:
# It's All Common to Man

*"Your existence is proof that God had a problem no one else can solve... You are Not Plan B!!!"*

–Dr. Mike Murdock

Ben set out on a trip to a part of the country he had never been. He loved cross-country driving and was careful along the hairpin bends and treacherous escarpments. The sky blue Toyota RAV4 roared along at his will, brand new tyres rumbling along the murram stretches. He would be there well before dark, he mused, as the greenery rushed wildly by.

It is an amazing success story. Looking at him now, no one would imagine that just two years before, Ben's shoes had holes for soles! He used a borrowed a mountain bike as his means of transport to and from work. One day his boss discovered the bike and literally went in stitches, laughing uncontrollably. Naturally the rest of the office joined in, totally embarrassing poor Ben. Bicycle jokes became the in-thing. Worse still, he got wet in the pouring rains and in the poor visibility he hit the side of a brand new pick-up truck. An ugly scar stretched across its side, badly ruining the paintwork. Ben had a nasty gash on his thigh and the bike was extensively damaged too. The driver was livid, and since he had to explain the damage to his stern boss, he forced Ben in, hurled the offending bike in the back and drove off in the opposite direction, a journey that took Ben several miles away from his work place!

Looking at Ben driving a new off-road four wheel-drive machine, you would not imagine that this potential filled-lad had at one time walked barefoot, lived in the village for more than a decade without any hope of ever stepping into a major town. Ben and his siblings had the unenviable task of fetching water daily for domestic use, and also to water their cattle (his father did not believe in taking the animals down to the river).

The first time Ben wore 'shoes' was after he had aced his Primary Leaving Examinations. He felt important. He had just transitioned into another phase in life, and to him, wearing bathroom sandals the whole day in the dusty village sort of raised his pedigree. You don't ace papers and walk barefoot, do you?

**Is there more to Life?**
The truth is that Ben did not even know himself at that time, or how many odds he had been up against in his life. Yet nobody can blame a thirteen year old for this. The opportunity came to join a prestigious boarding High School, and this was a defining moment for Ben, a journey of self-discovery. He had unconsciously become accustomed to the struggle with poverty. Yet, despite their low estate, Ben's family was one of the most 'well to do' in the village. His mother was the Deputy Headmistress at St. Lukes Primary School, the only local elementary school for miles around, and a pride to the humble community. His father was soon to be an ordained Minister of the gospel, another prestigious position by their standards. And so they were several ladders

higher than an average rural family.

> "It is not a strange thing that odds are the breeding grounds for greatness in life".

Ben did not know the odds his parents faced raising up four boys with meager earnings. He did not know that the illnesses he had suffered without proper medical care were great odds in a normal world. Everyone had settled and gotten accustomed to that way of life in the village…and so had Ben.

This notwithstanding, Ben was very competitive, a smart thinker and always wanting to win an argument. He always saw himself at the top of his class. This competitive trait, he did not know, would one day be pivotal in the affairs of his life.

---

*"When you are not in your assignment, you make life miserable for everyone around you"*
—Dr. Mike Murdock

---

He was blessed to be in a class of smart kids that gave him serious competition. The stakes were always higher each new term, and each new year. At best, Ben was always the fourth overall in the class. He topped the class once amidst the fierce competition, and did not hold that position again until the final examination in which he scored top marks.

It's All Common to Man

Talk about odds at any moment and you will realize that you have a company of close to seven billion people. There is no human being who did not have odds against them in their lives right from birth! Everyone born of a woman into planet earth must survive by screaming in the first few moments of introduction to life. Strangely enough, nurses and doctors get really excited about this cry. The reason as to why medics get so happy when a newborn is cries is that they know there is a sign of life there. It is an odd thing to those who would not know. *It is not a strange thing that odds are the breeding grounds for greatness in life!*

When Ben was growing up, he remembers his mum narrating the story of his elder brother Tim. This was an important hint in Ben's quest for essence of life. When Tim was born, according to their mum, he did not let out that all-important cry. She honestly thought that her first baby child was a still born. It was not until some minutes later that the new born baby cried out aloud, to the relief of mother and the medical staff.

Tim started out at school as a very smart boy, always at the top his class. However as years passed by, he grew slower and slower for no apparent reason. Chronic stagnation had set in. Most of his siblings went past him in Primary School. By the time Ben was doing his second year in High School, Tim had just managed to reach the final year of primary school. He unfortunately fell sick while Ben was on mid-term vacation. Ben had never been in a hospital before taking care of a sibling and this was his first time.

> *"At fourteen years of age, Ben was too afraid to face the worst head-on. Unfortunately, the lesson was not assimilated then and therefore checkered his life for years to come".*

> "What on earth would man do with himself if something didn't stand in the way?"
> —H.G. Wells

It was a moment of trauma for Ben, yet he had learnt to bolt down his fears. One day Ben went to the hospital to see Tim who was already being attended to by their mum. It rained so heavily that day that the road to the hospital was impassable, and so Ben was dropped off from the public transport van he had used close to three kilometers from the hospital and walked the rest of the journey there.

When he arrived, this fourteen year old boy went straight to his elder brother's ward. To his shock and dismay, he did not find his mother, nor his ailing brother! There were no mobile phones those days to call and locate. Ben was terrified and feared the worst. In fact, he did not want anybody to confirm his worst fear, which is why he never dared to ask the nurses on the whereabouts of his brother.

This seemingly small decision to *postpone* the inevitable has played a very key role in Ben's life, especially contributing to several instances in his life where he has been stuck. There is always that false comfort of not wanting to know, staying ignorant.

Very many people the world over fall in this category. They do not want to face their fears head on. To them, the revelation of reality or truth is a terror! They would rather frolic in the comfort offered by the period between the apprehension and the confirmation…otherwise known as waiting. So they find something to do, something to occupy them until the fear manifests itself. By this time, the situation at hand has deteriorated to monstrous proportions. At fourteen years of age, Ben was too afraid to face the worst head-on. Unfortunately, the lesson was not assimilated then and therefore checkered his life for years to come.

---

*"Fear has two meanings: Forget Everything and Run. Face Everything and Rise. The choice is yours"*
—Billy Cox

---

He left silently and walked back home in the muddy weather, something that was not a big deal now due to the impending major 'bad news'. At home, he never told anybody what he encountered at the hospital. He was pensive. He went to bed and stayed awake the whole night, waiting for a shriek that would announce the death of his brother, as was the custom in the village during those days. The dead body would usually be brought home for burial at night or in the wee hours of the morning.

So Ben waited for the commotion. He waited for the worst, and hoped for a miracle. His heart raced so fast that he was restless and deprived of sleep. How can one sleep under those conditions? Well, the only way you could have a sound sleep in the circumstance was if you did not *care*. Yet Ben did care, and he cared a lot. He must have dozed off once or twice and woke up with a start several times. Morning came and with it, Ben's Mum. She had come back home to check on how the boys at home were doing.

What a relief it was for Ben! There was no bad news. All was well. An ailing brother is better than a dead one, right? Ben narrated his ordeal to his mum and they exchanged those 'knowing' looks. To date, they never have discussed the tremendous trauma Ben went through, and never have they shared with anybody else, unless of course Ben's mum told his dad later on. His brother was discharged and came back home. Life seemed to move back to 'normal' as Ben returned to school for the second term.

One day at school, his former teacher and friend to his dad came visiting him from the village. He literally asked Ben to pack some of his stuff so that they could go home. Ben knew that something was amiss, but never in his wildest dreams could he imagine that Tim, his childhood friend and brother had gone, passed away. It was only when they drew close home that he was startled by the manner people greeted them as they passed…they were offering condolences.

So Ben got home and found a crowd of mourners peering into a dark brown coffin draped in white cloth. A large wreath of red roses stood somberly at the middle. His heart lurched violently within him. Tim was dead. The grief hurt so bad, Ben does not remember where the tears and the heavy sobbing came from. For some reason, he was the only one of his siblings that was *this* moved. He did not want to eat. He was devastated.

### The importance of Quality Questions
So here comes an opportunity to ask questions. An opportunity to ponder about life. Here comes a pivotal moment in this young lad's life to ponder on the real meaning of life. Oh what *odds* had *Tim* faced to date? Ben was so sorry that Tim did not make it. Tim actually did try so much. He had become a good artist and would progress in that department and see how it would be with him in life. Yet death came knocking, and now Tim was gone.

> *"In fact many a people's sole purpose of living is to swat away all these odds from their lives. What a useless and cruel vicious cycle"!*

In Ben's grief, he *wished* he would have been there with Tim. He wondered how it must have felt for Tim. Was he scared? Was he in pain? Was death painful? Did Tim think about Ben? Did he think about his own dreams? Oh, the devastation Ben felt! The emptiness! The odds in life are inescapable, and remotely, this one incident was one odd that Ben faced…just one amongst the many that are a sum total of this corporate executive.

And you know what? All these are common to man. All the odds, all the dips, disappointments, disillusionments, distresses, despondencies…they are all common to man. Every last one of us. In fact many a people's sole purpose of living is to swat away all these odds from their lives. What a useless and cruel vicious cycle!

That was the in the past.

Now, several years later, all these odds were forgotten…or automatically relegated to the periphery of the subconscious. Ben lives in an executive apartment, drives a nice car, and carries an impressive - smart phone—all property of the company he worked for. Life was good. Cash flow and liquidity were of less and less pressure. 'Out of the blue', Ben was earning four times better than his wildest dreams!

---

*"I discovered that to change the world I had to learn about myself while really engaging with my day-to-day relationships"*
~ Kim George

---

Ben had become so passionate about people and he loved to empower them. He looked forward to meeting his team. Money was not a problem. Fuel was not a problem. Rent was not even an issue, having been settled eight months in advance by his company. Or so Ben thought. Does life really consist of mastering the basic needs of food, clothing and shelter?

Food was not a problem. Medical care was not a problem. He would comfortably pay dialysis fees for his younger brother. He would save at least a good amount of his earnings monthly. Here was a man who was living a good dream. Still, he knew that he had not yet arrived. He hoped for more. He looked forward for more progress, more abundance, more success. He knew about significance in life. He craved to live, love and matter…he just knew that there had got to be much more to life than what he was experiencing.

Yet in his corporate position, Ben was comfortable. The call to find out his more was now becoming benign: a mere backdrop that does not abuse the senses.

Ben has had his fair share of *awakenings.* These came ostensibly to arouse Ben to what really matters. That is what life does to us. *There will always be this restlessness we all will have until we finally start living what matters. Otherwise, life is a ruthless burden.*

The problem is that a vast majority of people have learnt and become good professionals at avoiding the awakening calls of life. A death in the family, a parent's job loss, shattered dreams, some scaring ailment, an eviction, a separation, a divorce, retrenchment and any other hardship that life throws at us.

> *"Truly, mankind must learn that we are living in a dark and fallen world. Our response in such times of catastrophe should inspire us to ask the correct questions".*

> *"Social stagnation results not from a lack of answers but from the absence of the impulse to ask questions"*
> —Erick Hoffer

Truly, mankind must learn that we are living in a dark and fallen world. Our response in such times of catastrophe should inspire us to ask the correct questions. Sadly, most people ask these why questions more than the useful what and how questions. Indeed, the why questions come naturally and can linger over time.

We would however do ourselves much better service if we learnt to move on from those questions and start asking empowering questions— powerful "how" and "what" questions.

For Example, a young family suffers the loss of a husband and dad, and bread winner. Instead of asking *"Why did God have to let him die..."* they can now ask, *"Now that Dad is no longer with us, how can we effectively maintain our daily sustenance?"* An answer to the latter question is more powerful than the former. In fact, sometimes there are no answers to such why questions, at least this side of eternity.

**And here is the biggest thing to note: How about learning to ask such a question even *before* dad departs? Herein ladies and gentlemen, is one of the biggest blows against being 'stuck': *asking questions that make you to be ahead of time.***

It is being proactive. We could never play God Almighty, and I know that as much as we would want to be proactive, life would still throw us a curveball from time to time. Yet when it does, if we had *perceived* it through anticipatory questions, we would have bought ourselves some time. *Perception is not just a spiritual gift; perception can also be a fruit that comes from the discipline of asking the correct questions.*

> *"Instead of "Why did God have to let him die..." we can now ask, "Now that Dad is no longer with us, how can we effectively maintain our daily sustenance?" An answer to the latter question is more powerful than the former. In fact, sometimes there are no answers to such why questions, at least this side of eternity".*

**The Meaning of Life**
Like everybody, Ben, at his formative years had wondered about the meaning of life. There is no one on the face of the earth who is not accorded this opportunity to ponder about the meaning of life. Every one of us from every race, creed, nationality, tribe, tongue and color and religious persuasions have had that chance to ponder about the meaning of life.

Yet one of the biggest thieves of such meaningful moments has always been scheduled activities. One of our greatest needs as human beings is the need of being certain. So the easiest way of being certain has always been to craft tight schedules that we follow religiously. From birth to marriage, a carefully crafted plan has been identified the world-over. Once an individual has gone successfully through this cycle, they meticulously pass it on to the next generation!

> *"The quality of your life is in direct proportion to the amount of uncertainty you can comfortably live with"*
> —Tony Robbins

It is a vicious cycle that enslaves thousands upon thousands of people from all over the world in this meaningless schedule of life. A vast majority have, through this scheduling, successfully killed off the essence of life. Yet life never gives up. Life has been designed to have real meaning, and as long as we are incongruent with our fundamental nature, life will keep sending us signals of all kinds, reminding us of our broken focus.

> *"Sometimes dreams get buried by jobs that are unfulfilling, situations that are unraveling, "to do" lists that are unending, and finances that are overwhelming. When our attention is on all the "stuff" in life, our dreams get stifled."*
> —Erik Reese, S.H.A.P.E.

A vast majority of students out of universities are looking for scheduled activities packaged in one name—a job. *There is no problem with having a job or looking for one. There is a problem, however, in not searching for the meaning of life while relentlessly hunting for a job.* Ben has done this over and over again. Sometimes these jobs are just about anything that comes by.

There was this time that Ben had been enrolled by his dad in an employment agency just after College. Opportunities would come and Ben would rush there. One opportunity came where a particular client wanted a college graduate and insisted on computer literacy as a requirement. Ben was gleeful as he knew he qualified. He dressed up in his best second hand two piece suit and dashed for the interview.

> *There was no word for Ben from God. Not even an acknowledgement that Ben existed! Nothing! That shook Ben so heavily.*

After a mock interview, this multinational oil organization gives Ben an opportunity to work. Surprisingly, Ben was given a white overall and dust masks and assigned to a young lady who took him to a dusty, dark and abandoned cellar at the company's premises. His job? To look for papers in files that had a particular phrase! The multinational company was being sued and so they needed some historical evidence from their recycle bins.

Ben wondered! Why on earth did they need a College Graduate with good computer skills for that? Ben remembers one moment when the lady he was working with had stepped out. He broke down and sobbed heavily. He wondered: Is this it, Lord? Is this all there is in life? Is this the use of my sixteen years in school? A few days' job in a dusty cellar in a multinational oil company?

> *"Job security is gone. The driving force of a career must come from the individual. Remember: Jobs are owned by the company. You own your career!"*
> — Earl Nightingale

Yet you should see how excited people get when they are shortlisted for interviews—any interview. It is a moment of breakthrough! All that they have been doing is waiting for that phone to ring. Waiting for the email to come in. Waiting for the word of mouth. Waiting for a connection from a friend or a relative!

Ben was smack in the middle of this group, a very faithful subscriber, if you will. That moment where he was sobbing and asking *"Is this it?"* was another hint in his life. Yet as I have described in another book, **'Permission for Greatness: Bridging the Gap between School and Relevance'**, Ben lacked the capacity to 'manage his transitions'. And so that golden moment slipped by as he started chasing for his payment from this temporary job...and ultimately started waiting for another opportunity to get *another* interview! Oh the waiting that the masses must be doing the world over!

> *"Nothing is more torturous than waiting for others to change so you can succeed"*
> –Dr. Mike Murdock

You can see that Ben was stuck at that time. There is no doubt about that. Like we have seen, every moment a stuck situation comes by, it is an opportunity to reflect. It is a chance to evaluate. It is a powerful hint that we might not be focusing on what we need to be focusing on.

The closest Ben came to really do something about his meaning in life was a bit earlier on.

When Ben was 17 he had the opportunity to think about his real meaning and to search it out. His elder brother [Gerald] at Campus went missing, unbeknown to everyone in the family. Apparently, he went 'out of his senses', boarded a van that took him to a mountainous location where many people prayed. He stayed there for a period of three days until he came to his senses.

That whole debacle shook the entire family including Ben. His elder brother had become a Christian few years earlier. Ben had not joined the bandwagon, although he also had his fare share of convictions. What really came out as a highlight is when Ben's Dad invited some spiritually mature people to pray with the family after that scary drama with Ben's brother. Ben always felt awkward in such meetings and so he became evasive, and preferred to get into the kitchen to prepare tea.

> *"It is in the realm of uncertainty that your passion is found"*
> —Tony Robbins.

However, the visitors called for Ben. They wanted the whole family members present to attend the prayer session. Somewhere during that prayer, both Ben's dad and his elder brother got their prophecies, supposedly from God through this praying party.

There was no word for Ben from God. Not even an acknowledgement that Ben existed! Nothing! That shook Ben so heavily. It is at that moment that the real quest for his essence began. Indeed, this quest has been one of the longest that he has ever had in his life. It has been one of his deepest desires to know his fundamental nature.

At that time, the easiest way Ben thought to get his own message from God was to join the spiritual people. With great conviction, which of course had been always coming to him, largely due to exposure, Ben decided to join the Christian faith. This was a momentous occasion in his life. Yet this still did not answer the why question of Ben's life.

Yet again, the trap of activities and schedules even in religion can easily become an anesthesia to the all critical quest of finding our '*why*'. So life moved on for Ben, though he was never the same again. His quest was totally spiritual. Ben displays total loyalty, commitment and zeal, ingredients that work quickly with spirituality. Whenever people like Ben land somewhere, they give all their gut and commitment to that place.

> *"You must be a hunter of uncertainty…the more you pursue it, the stronger you become"*
> —Tony Robbins

That is exactly what Ben did for more than a decade after his spiritual encounter. By the time Ben was taking this trip, his quest had hit an overdrive. He was hungrier. He still sought to know his purpose. That is not to say that he was entirely uncomfortable. No. Ben was enjoying what life had given him so far. It is the realization that he was smarter than the people around him that fueled the craving for his purpose in life again.

Just like the road Ben was on today, life is also filled with twists and turns, bumps and potholes, crazy drivers who want to compete, prideful truck drivers who could not care less for other people's safety. Indeed, anything is bound to happen to us when we are on the journey of life. That is what makes it exciting and adventurous.

Ben was now hundreds of miles out of city and well into the country-side. He couldn't be happier with himself. He finally got the chance to rendezvous with one of his team members, based 200 miles away from the city. He felt excited about this, and the prospect of covering the entire country with such trips energized and excited him tremendously. In exactly three hours after he had set off, Ben arrived at the very first location under his field team's jurisdiction. Here, he met with one young man that he had employed immediately after an interview for the then vacant position. His name was Mark. Mark had excited the panelists including Ben at the interview. He cut this aura of confidence and fun around him. He did not hesitate to joke about his salary expectation, leaving the panelists in stitches.

In all his life to that point in time, Ben had attended several interviews for different job positions. Ben had read extensively on how to behave at interviews…how hard you are to shake the hands of the panelists, how you need to smile, how you need to ask them some tough questions of your own. None of these things ever worked for Ben.

In fact, they were mere masks that made Ben's authenticity to look so plastic and imagined. This was pretty much unlike Mark, who was so comfortable in his skin. He was so in touch with himself. There was no hint of desperation in Mark's disposition. Up until now, Ben has choked up on several hours of experience being part of an interviewing panel. Now he knows that employers are not looking for supermen. They look for human beings who are first au-

> *"Employers are not looking for supermen. They are looking for human beings who are first authentic, and then who have the capacity to deliver. Not the other way round".*

thentic, and then who have the capacity to deliver. Not the other way round.

By the way, over the years, Ben had grown a knack of employing people who did not have the academic papers to prove that they are geniuses. A case in point is two individuals that Ben hired who never completed high school. These two were hired alongside a host of University graduates, yet when the work was being done, there was no hint of their lack of education. In fact, when Ben was out of the picture, a certain national company hired these two and overlooked the dozens others who had degrees!

> *"He was so stuck that it was his landlord who fed him from time to time, amidst asking diplomatically for rent that had not been paid for more than three months. How Ben got out of this situation is a story for another day, with several rich lessons that will be derived".*

Ben himself had been seriously stuck in the degree trap. He never had the chance to go to University and earn a degree. His parents could not pay for two kids at the University in the same year. So Ben ended up in a tertiary institution, a place where he ravenously 'ate up' the books in the library to the astonishment of many of his colleagues. He was simply hungry for information.

After two years in the Tertiary Institution and having earned a Higher Diploma, Ben went through a series of life curves, being stuck in the village once again before finally landing a job as an IT Consultant and Instructor in a Tertiary College. As it is of a seeker, he was again probing everything in that place to familiarize himself and add to his pedigree. Not before long, Ben was an asset at that place.

---

*"To live is the rarest thing on earth. Most people just exist"*
~ Oscar Wilde

---

However, after three years doing the same thing over and over again, Ben got tired! The beckoning of life's essence was knocking on the door again. He knew it. He still knew that he was meant for greater and mightier things than the mundane mechanical ruts that he was dispensing every six days in a week from 7:00 am to 8:00 pm.

One day, there was an opportunity for an interview that Ben took. He performed well and thought he would land that job. Throwing all caution to the wind, Ben resigned from his first job! As it turned out however, he was not successful. He waited for that job for weeks on end, until when he mailed the organization that effectively informed him of his failure to pass the interview.

Here was a man that was out of his parents' house, living on his own trying to make ends meet and live the essence of life. He was now jobless, yet with financial obligations. Ben was effectively stuck once again! He was so stuck that it was his landlord who fed him from time to time, amidst asking diplomatically for rent that had not been paid for more than three months. How Ben got out of this situation is a story for another day, with several rich lessons that will be derived.

Mark showed Ben a nice place where he could take some rest as they awaited the Team Leader for that part of the country. Mark loved to see Ben so much. He knew that Ben never had an attitude of lording it over his team members, but rather loved to inspire them. Mark was obviously confident of the job he had been doing.

A few minutes after he had a sumptuous meal, Ben was ready to explore this market for potential with Mark and his Team Leader. Ben loved working, and everyone in the organization knew that. Mark was to be left behind as the Team Leader and Ben explored the market. They would not proceed deeper into the interior of the country for that day. It was getting late by the hour and Ben never likes driving at night.

In the evening, after another sumptuous meal, Ben called it a day for that day. He retired to a Hotel that his Team Leader had helped book, reflected on the events of the day and planned for the next day. He was a thankful man. He was also on fire. He enjoyed what he was doing. He was adding value while in the field and while at the office. Man comes alive when he is engaged in something rewarding. If the next three years or so would be just like this year has turned out, our Corporate Executive would have a very rewarding life or so he thought.

That Ben was astute was not in question. That he was organized and cared deeply about his team was not a doubt to anybody.

In fact, Ben got into bad books with mirror members of the client organization that he was working for. He was 'way up there' according to them. His passion and drive threatened their complacency. His spontaneous contributions at brain storming sessions during board meetings stunned even himself.

Yet these events were happening to a man who was on a roll. Just the very previous year, Ben was sitting in an obscure office at the head office of his company as a data analyst. To make things worse, Ben was a victim of intimidation by his superior. He was on the firing line, literally, because his immediate supervisor had poisoned the CEO's mind with false allegations.

> *"Busyness is behavior driven by the belief that our worth is tied to how much we accomplish that can be seen by others".*
> —Kim George

In the CEO's eyes, Ben was rude, lazy, uncaring and always the first out of work at exactly five in the evening. The CEO wants people who are hardworking, people who can go up to midnight to help the company. Indeed, such people like Ben's supervisors did exist. Yet their going on to midnight was not due to their hard work, but due to their dumbness. This fact was illustrated physically to the CEO who later on realized how indeed Ben was of a different crop.

So here we have a man whose pedigree was an all time low just months before this current job. Having been elevated four scales down the pecking order to be an expatriate, Ben was definitely on a roll. His self esteem was an all time high. His belief in his capacity as a solutions man was being authenticated on a daily basis. You cannot fail to be excited when this bubble in your life happens. You savor it. You leverage on it. You ride the tide. You maximize the moment. You make the most use of the chance.

That is what Ben did. Unfortunately, this had its side effects. Members of the client organization were now openly opposed to Ben's company in their country. Relationships between Ben's company and the client organization became difficult.

If you have not noticed, all these 'downs' that have been happening to Ben have not been useless. In fact, some of these downs are serious red flags for Ben to come back to the drawing board of his life and ask those questions: "Am I living, Am I Loving, Do I Matter?"

> *"You must first be who you really are, then, do what you need to do, in order to have what you want"*
> —Margaret Young

## When work speaks louder than endearments

Just nine months before Ben was made one of the very first expatriate consultants for his company, he was summoned to the CEO's office. Out of the blue, the CEO wanted Ben out. Yet, according to the CEO, there was something that kept Ben from being fired. Something the CEO could not put a finger on.

*"Ben, I want you to know that I came to this office at the beginning of this year with a purpose to let you go. You have a bad attitude and I will not condone it".*

Ben was shell-shocked to say the least. Consciously, he never thought himself as being rude. The CEO did not as much give Ben any time to defend or explain himself. In fact, according to Ben, he was dealt with as if you would deal with a dangerous viper! Ben was nearly reduced to tears at the CEO's office because all the allegations against him were false and far-fetched. Unbeknown to him, he

> *"It is in the moments of strife and pressure that the true character of people is revealed. Ben was downcast to say the least. Previously, he would be so cozy in conversing with his CEO, now he was numb".*

was a pawn in someone's chess board who wanted favor in the eyes of the CEO at his expense. Unfortunately for him, the chess master had the CEO's ear and trust…Ben had neither!

"I do not know what is keeping me from firing you Ben, but this is what will happen: I am putting you on three months probation where you will only draw half your salary. If I do not see any improvement in you, then we will part ways!" That was the CEO's verdict.

Just to make it more difficult for Ben, it was immediately decided that he takes up the responsibilities of his colleague who had a massive history of leaving work at midnight and staying on late into the weekends. Any casual observer would say that Ben's colleague was a hard working individual, no doubt about that. According to Ben's detractors, his goose was well cooked!

Yet it is in the moments of strife and pressure that the true character of people is revealed. Ben was downcast. Previously, he would be so cozy in conversing with his CEO, now he was numb. The days that followed, he behaved like a scared pupil in the headmaster's office. Every encounter with the CEO was awkward.

But that is not to say that all was that bad. It took Ben just two days to learn the ropes of what his colleague used to do. Ben had resigned to the prospect of leaving work at midnight every day. Yet as Ben studied his new responsibilities, the more he dispensed them, the more he realized that there must be a better way of doing things.

> *"Thomas Carlyle said "Nothing is more terrible than activity without insight". Actually, I can think of something equally terrible and that is insight without activity".*
> ~ Kim George

Coming out of a strong IT background albeit without a degree, Ben automatically decided to have most of his work automated. We need to learn and understand that for the most part, we will get unstuck from challenging situations using what we already posses, seldom what lies out there that we have no grasp over.

Guess what happened? With his new automated system, Ben was able to do a better job, produce better reports and still leave work at five in the evening! On the other hand, Ben's colleague was grappling with what used to be Ben's work. The result is that the company's clients bitterly complained of the lateness and shallow quality of work.

### From prison to palace: The road of excellence

Ben was vindicated. There was even a day that this same Ben's colleague went on a two-week's leave. Ben not only dispensed his duties, but also his colleagues with so much finesse, and he still would leave work at exactly five sharp to go practice for theatre since he was a budding thespian! At one point, Ben was tempted to ask the organization that was threatening to let go of one of his colleagues not to employ a replacement, but transfer those responsibilities to him alongside the paycheck. He knew he would handle it!

> *Do you see a man skillful in his work? He will stand before kings; he will not stand before obscure men.*
> —Proverbs 22:29

In addition, the Company's clients got an opportunity to see Ben's work first hand and even wished that they had such level of organization on their end. They immediately requested for Ben to be available at their offices at least twice each week.

The CEO would have none of it, finally realizing Ben's value. This was not done through campaigning and calling the boss at midnight just to show that one was working as was the manner with some. There was now a tug of war between the CEO and the company's client over Ben. His value had just gone up. That was a massive come-back! This was the best thing ever in Ben's corporate world.

Once again, Ben was on top of the world. He loved what he was doing, adding value to his work and ultimately to himself. In fact, when he took over from his colleague, he wrote to the client and told them that he would totally change the way a certain report was written. The client asked for a trial of the same before they could approve it. The product was so fine that the client was embarrassed of what they had previously issued as a report template.

So as you can see, great things were happening in his life. He had depended on his landlord for food but now was making things happen at a grand level. Ben had become indispensable. It did not take much time thereafter that an international client came knocking seeking expertise. Ben's company was their choice.

The CEO could not look past Ben, who was four scales down the pecking order (A total of 52 people ahead of him) for promotion! It is this same CEO that had turned down Ben's request to be a Team Leader. Ben had passionately known that he could do a wonderful job in that position. He had interfaced with other Team Leaders and they could report to him on some matters. Their conduct told Ben that what they were doing was not rocket science and that he would do it even better. The CEO said NO.

So now that his pedigree had grown through leaps and bounds, Ben did not even have to apply for this position. He did not even have an idea that there was this kind of position. He was busy working when the CEO called him to his office and literally begged him to take up the new position!

> *"Life and nature abhors a straight line"*
> —Antony Robbins

So here was Ben, seemingly having 'arrived' as it were. A happy lad he was as he took up his new position. The more Ben got closer and closer to his purpose, the more and more he kept asking. We should remember that our essence mostly never just shows up in total package, wrapped up with an instruction manual. That happened to guys like Moses of Mt. Sinai, and even then, it took him a whooping 80 years!

We get hints in life to show us that we are homing in on our essence. The clues can be very easy. Sometimes it is something that excites us, something we are passionate about, something wrong that totally infuriates us, or even something we dream about daily.

## The Trap of Familiarity and Presumption
For Ben, he had stumbled into something that excited him. He had loved

> "So now that his pedigree had grown through leaps and bounds, Ben did not even have to apply for this position. He did not even have an idea that there was this kind of position".

researching about leadership. Indeed, he had been a trained leader at his local church. Out of the many possible candidates, Ben was once chosen as a team leader to a Prison Blitz, a countrywide outreach to all the prisons in three days that the church was undertaking throughout his country. Here was a lad in his early twenties leading a team of 80 church people to one of the most notorious maximum prison in his country! Now, that was a major hint!

Unfortunately we take such hints for granted. If your father was the president, it would still be easy to take him for granted. People the world over would be admiring him for what a great visionary he is, yet to you, he is *just* dad. Presumption. Conceit. Familiarity.

The same happens with what we are passionate about . Look at the following examples:   in his book 'The Coming Wealth Transfer, Matthew Ashimolowo states the following:

> The Mail on Sunday, a British newspaper on April 16th 2006 listed six people who had great ideas but never really made much of it and never profited from it. Software genius **Gary Gildall** invented the first operating system for a personal computer. However, when invited for a meeting with IBM, he went flying. Bill Gates went on to sell his own MSDOS, the rest is history.
>
> **Kane Kramer**, a British gentleman designed and sketched out the first iPod in 1979 but did nothing with it. Today the iPod has taken over the world. He remains a store man at a furniture showroom in Hertfordshire, England—Matthew Ashimolowo, 'Coming Wealth Transfer'

For the most part, no doubt, these people took for granted what they possessed as concepts. We cannot over-emphasize this point. It will be important for us to see how Ben was plagued later on in his life by the trap that is the familiar.

"Familiarity breeds contempt" is a familiar saying

Ladies and Gentlemen, the biggest lesson I have learnt in the first quarter of my life is this: There is a place for everyone's passion in this world. However queer, irrelevant, weird and pitiful it might seem to others, as long as that passion comes from deep down the core of your heart and spirit, there is a place for it in the world.

One big problem that dreamers and master visionaries face in the initial stages of life is this: the validity of their dreams. You find them always wondering...how will it look like in the real world? And so you find someone looking down on an idea that they have because they think it will not be accepted in this world. But a vision is a vision. It is much better for it to be weird and done than to be cute and undone.

> *"We always think that what matters is something spectacular. Something that we have sweated to find. Something rare. Some gemstone. Some 'secret'. In life however, real meaning is commonly found on the surface and easily overlooked".*

That being said, there is another major trap that plagues very many people. This is what I have called the 'trap of the familiar'. If you remember the story of Jesus Christ, you would notice that He could not perform miracles in is home town. Why? The trap of that which is familiar kept His folk from believing that He was more of a Miracle Worker than a carpenter's son.

> *"WHEN first the Fox saw the Lion he was terribly frightened, and ran away and hid himself in the wood. Next time however he came near the King of Beasts he stopped at a safe distance and watched him pass by. The third time they came near one another the Fox went straight up to the Lion and passed the time of day with him, asking him how his family were, and when he should have the pleasure of seeing him again; then turning his tail, he parted from the Lion without much ceremony".*
>
> FAMILIARITY BREEDS CONTEMPT—The Harvard Classics, The Fox and the Lion (Fables of Aesop)

The trap of that which is familiar works every day, and creeps up on us, stealing our ideas and dreams. This is how it works: You get this passion or this idea about something...but the fact that 'you did not sweat it', you kind of think "Arrgh...what the heck, it is *only* a thought".

For some reason, we expect to work, sweat, with smoke coming out of our ears because of serious thinking, before we can take an idea seriously. I have had some writings done in the recent past that I thought, *"Oh well, I just filled up some space today...I didn't feel that post at all!"*...only to get positive comments, thanking me for that very post that I thought had no place. Oh! The trap of the familiar! At some point in time, I did not post a single message on my blog for weeks, until I started receiving phone calls and emails, people asking, "What's up? You don't write no more?"

We expect to follow something because it is grandiose...but we shun the important things that resonate with our hearts, since they do not have any signs we think of as greatness. Writers would relate with this: Have you ever gone back to your 'drawing board' or 'recycle bin' and re-read some of the things you were toying with? You normally exclaim! I have asked myself sometimes, "Whoa, who in the world was that writing? What was he thinking? Was that me?" I am exclaiming at stuff that I have unearthed from my rubbish bin!

It is time to restore some files from the 'recycle bin' people. Look, if it matters to you, I guarantee you that it matters to the world. There is a place for it in this world. It could very well be the basis of your *Life Signatures*. Think about it for a moment...do you receive these mighty ideas of revolution on a daily basis? Hardly! In fact, if you do not take charge of the small 'familiar' ideas you have already received, you start losing the 'IDEAS.FM' network.

One of the most dangerous killers of potential and dreams is that thing called *presumption*. People do nothing because they presume. People let down their guard because they presume. People presume because they are too familiar with their idea or potential. Presuming people especially on their own selves end up being so scornful of what they end up seeing in the market place what was once their ideas...and worse still, they still do nothing. This leads to absolute contempt, seeing only the negatives in something than the positive potential it has.

 Friend, could there be death in your life because of familiarity? Could presumption be wasting away your skills, potential, dreams, vision? Only you can find out.

As for now, Ben's 'more' was not yet clear to him yet it lay on the surface for everyone to see. It was like an invisible magnet that was pulling him towards this noble direction. Yet he was not sure if he knew the path to take. He was not sure if it depended on his efforts alone. He did not know if the divine would unfold it to him miraculously, or if he would stumble on the 'more' accidentally.

He always knew he was meant for better things…and much better than that, he even felt 'called' to be a major catalyst in his generation. Here is a man with corporate gadgets who knows he is called, but is not clear about the call. Here is a man who knows he was meant to make a difference sometime later in the future in a major way.

> "The illusions are like a fog that very slowly settles over us. Before long, the darkened view ahead seems normal. We forget that only a few feet above us is clear sky. Some people walk their entire lives in this fog, never questioning the source or nature of the fog, and rarely risking the safety of the fog to poke their heads out, if even for a moment"
> —Kim George.

Yet one wonders how many 'Bens' are out there. One wonders how many have this sense of urgency, this pull towards their 'more'. Still one wonders how many are clearly on that path, the only path that they were meant to take…the path of living their 'more.'

> One big problem that dreamers and master visionaries face in the initial stages of life is this: the Validity of their dreams. You find them always wondering…'how will it look like in the real world'?

Early the following morning, Ben and his Team Leader started the day off with a heavy breakfast. The next few hours were then spent inspecting the aspects of the Client's business in that region. It was in the mid morning that Ben and his Team Leader set off to their next market area, some 150 Miles away.

The journey was spent with Ben enquiring more and more about the business in the market. Ben gathered crucial information from the team leader in terms of recommendations that he would give to his superior as well as the client. He knew that he needed to be careful with this. The last time he made such a comprehensive report, there was a serious backlash. Apparently the client's representative in the reported region felt undermined and exposed. He felt as if the report insinuated that he was not working. Obviously, he shared his sentiments with his colleagues who in turn felt that their jobs were in danger if they continued to rest on their laurels.

> *Feedback is the breakfast of champions*
> —Brian Tracy

Yet Ben, a thorough worker, knew that the information from the ground was exactly what the companies needed to make smart decisions. He took a mental note on being wise the next time he would create such a report in order to avoid the backlash.

Interestingly enough, the questions between Ben and his Team Leader were just one-sided. How sad! It was only Ben who was asking the questions. We have to notice that in life, the askers normally become more enlightened. In the previous similar trip, another Team Leader was smart enough to ask Ben how he managed to land such a lucrative position in such an esteemed company.

Ben did not hide. Ben told him how he was an obscure data analyst in the immediate previous post. This wise Team Leader listened intently. The current Team Leader in Ben's trip did not take that advantage. This is where very many people come short. Someone finds themselves in a very rare presence of an influencer and cannot gather courage to ask relevant questions.

**One is always better than you; yet you are always better than someone**
Books have been written on various topics. The shortcut to getting such information at no cost directly from the horse's mouth has always been presented to people…yet very few take advantage of this grand opportunity. You see, we are all sandwiches if you will. It does not matter where you come from, your color, religion, creed, nation or background. It does not matter your financial, social, or physical status. You my friend are a sandwich! Yes, you read that right. Sandwich.

Here is what I mean.

I was out one day jogging when I met two types of people, and both of them were jogging too. The first guy was going my opposite direction. Concerning him, I was able to reach my turning point, come back and basically overtake him! *insert smiley here!*

The second guy, I have 'met' before. Actually we did not meet…no, he actually zoomed past me like some professional athlete (by the way…maybe he is). On this latest occasion however, we actually met, as he was jogging my opposite direction.

I shouted at him, 'Mister, we have to talk one of these fine days!'

He shouted back, "Alright man."

It will be interesting to see what will come out of that conversation, I honestly can't wait!

---

*"Effectiveness occurs when your actions are in alignment with your purpose, vision, and values".*
—Kim George

Here is the main thing. The first guy we talked about earlier was and still is so slow to such an extent that I can beat him any day any time. The second guy is so fast he can beat me hands down. Right there is the whole recipe for a Sandwich! You see, there is always going to be someone better than you in anything you are doing. There will also be someone a lot worse than yourself in what your pursuits. You are a Sandwich, get it now?

But get this straight. My success is not measured in how easily I build rings around the slowest in my niche...my success is actually measured by how fast I am able to catch up with the niche pace setter and overtake them! In other words, to really measure the strides I am making, the yardstick is a sandwich with the focus on the leader and not the follower. I have realized that if I am a speaker, there are better speakers than myself. If I am a footballer, there are better footballers than myself...the same applies with writing, cooking, or virtually any area of passion. TD Jakes said that if you only surround yourself with people who ONLY want to learn from you....then you are not growing.

> *"In life, we ought to know the two members of our 'sandwich team', and know whom we can easily benefit from".*

*Here is the thing though....you are only a sandwich if you are in motion.* Outside of motion, you are not even in the game. Two things happen in motion. Either, we are fleeing...or we are pursuing! From what I have learnt thus far, I'd rather be in hot pursuit than in terrified flight!

So here is what I have decided to do...that just like I have sought audience with the second guy, I will always want to be in the presence of my superiors. I have no problem accepting the fact that there is someone better than me. I have also noticed that these gurus or market leaders are so enlightened that they are only happy to share their 'secrets' of being on top of their game.

So, I want to find out these: Why does the second guy run that fast? Why does he jog daily in the first place? Who is he? What does he do? What does he want in life?

Look, there is more than 90% chance that the second guy is making changes in his area of influence. There is also absolute certainty that the first guy is on top of his peers especially if they do not have a personal challenge like he does against himself. You know why? Both these guys are in motion!

Most importantly, the Sandwich himself, after realizing that pursuit is far much stronger than flight, he will certainly improve day by day. You need both. We need the first guy so that we are not demoralized or discouraged with what we are doing. We however need the second guy to keep us in check and to help us not let conceit into our heads.

Take some time today and find out…who is your 'first guy'? Who is your 'second guy'? Make a list of your second guys and endeavor to get smack in the middle of their circles of influence.

---

*"Deep within man dwell those slumbering powers; powers that would astonish him, that he never dreamed of possessing; forces that would revolutionize his life if aroused and put into action."*
—Orison Swett Marden

---

So, Ben's second Team Leader either dared not to ask of Ben the issues of life or he flatly decided not to. Maybe it never occurred to him that he should. He missed his opportunity. It is not surprising later on that when Ben was not in the picture, this Team Leader was fired off of his job in just a few weeks. Where did he go? To date, Ben does not have a clue. *It is common to man that if we do not change the direction of our lives after some 'awakenings', we might be stuck forever.*

Granted, we might not even know we are stuck…or worse yet, we simply get accustomed to that kind of a stuck life like Ben did while at the village. The biggest key to unlock mysteries is to pose consistent curious and meaningful questions. When we stop to ask, we stop to grow. We all know of the success of Google, an internet search engine. Every single moment, someone is searching for something. And you know what? *The seekers always find. It is just a matter of time.*

> *"My success is not measured in how easily I build rings around the slowest in my niche… my success is actually measured by how fast I am able to catch up with the niche pace setter"!*

Ladies and Gentlemen, it is true that there is one paramount thing that is common to man. For it is true of human nature, that there is a void inside all of us, that can only be filled when we finally set our feet on that high road of life's purpose. What will matter in the end should be what matters right now.

Brendon Burchard, the Founder of Experts Academy says it this way,

"In the end, did I live, did I love or did I matter?"

Looking at the path that Ben's life has taken so far, it would be intriguing to answer all those important questions. Is he living?

How do you define living? Is living having a job, a company car, staying in an exquisite house that is paid by the company months upfront and owning sophisticated communication gadgets belonging to the company? Is living having the capacity to pay bills comfortably? How do you measure the quality of a life well lived? Better yet, how do you determine right now that the life one is living is of good quality?

Like I have already said, in life, questions are answers. We ought to learn that our state of being stuck mostly is unlocked by asking the right questions, and being courageous enough to immediately act on the answers that always will come.

## LESSONS FROM BEN
Taking a cross-sectional look at the life of Ben till now, there are pertinent lessons that we can glean and apply.

The major lesson here is that the several dips of life are a pre-set appointment to every human being. This is dictated by two major factors: First, we are human and we have our limits, regardless of advancement in technology. Second, we live and interact with a fallen and imperfect world. There is no human being in the face of the earth that is not susceptible to failure, stress, despondency, lack, distress, betrayal, misfortune, bereavement and the myriads of negatives that are common to man. Our action point here is to take a mental note and discover that we are creatures of resilience, right from before conception. Everyone has a story of their own to tell. Yet as much as we are appointed to trouble as sure as the sparks fly upwards, we have been pre-packaged with mighty doses or resilience in us that can virtually see us through any obstacle that comes our way. Such is the calling of man. My definition of success is "The continuous process of challenge mastery"

There are two major types of people: There are those who know their purpose and direction in life to the greatest of clarity. There are also those who do not know their essence in life albeit having their schedules full to capacity with iterating activities. Both parties are prone to experience moments of being stuck.

The quest of knowing our essence in life is inherent in every soul regardless of their status in society. Even a madman in the streets does have that beckon in their life to live, love and matter. The greatest folly in a massive percentage of the human population is to fill our schedules with activities while unknowingly silencing that beckoning in our lives. Sadly, as far as having a real and intended impact on earth, many humans are stuck. Ultimately, when life throws us the curve balls, they suffer greatly who have systematically silenced their beckonings. Our lesson here is to be truer to ourselves and show up to our beckon than ever before.

It is in asking the right questions that we will clarify our purpose in life. We ought to be more intentional in asking than reactionary. We ought to be deeper in asking than whining. We ought to ask more of the how questions than we do the why questions. We ought to be forward looking regardless of the unfavorable circumstances surrounding us instead of trying to find out who is responsible for our condition.

There is no event whether good or bad that is useless to man. Every experience we go through is connected to our resilience index, however remote t may seem.. Even the most unlikely bad, traumatizing event has a way of forming a basis for leading us towards our true selves if we are keen enough to ask the right questions.

The beauty of life is the journey itself, and not necessarily the destination. We ought to be more alive during the journey than we are at the destination. The bulk of life is in processes, not at the destinations.

When faced with a situation that threatens you to be stuck, it is important to ask the right questions. These questions must address who we really are as well as where we are going. For the most part, people ask 'why me?' Others choose to ask better questions like 'how can we get out of here'. Yet the best questions to ask are 'who am I?', and 'where am I going?' A stuck situation in life which is common to man is an opportunity for us to know exactly the answers to those questions. To be unstuck, make sure you have the appropriate answers to these two questions. These are vision questions. If you take a man with a vision and put him in the desert, and he will survive. Vision is absolutely critical for survival. Take a man with no vision and place him right in the middle of abundance, and he will die. When stuck, a man must make sure that their essence is not shaken or watered down, but reaffirmed. When stuck, a man should make sure to revisit their vision and clarify it. A man should make sure that he remains true to his vision. Any attempt to escape the crisis without employing a visionary approach will only aggravate the bad situation further deepen that crisis.

# CHAPTER 2:

# What Causes People to get Stuck?

*"Problems are a sign of life, the more you got, the more life you have"*

–Norman Vincent Peale

One thing we need to be aware of is that every individual is an ordinary person with the capacity of living an extra-ordinary life. Some people would actually tell us that we are all already extra-ordinary, with the potential of experiencing the extra-ordinary life. There is some truth in that. The only problem is that we all seldom realize the 'extra-ordinary' that we are. The moment we grasp the message that we are 'extra-ordinary', then the extra ordinary life can be experienced. This realization or knowledge is critical especially when hardship comes knocking.

Looking at the life of Ben, we realize how 'common' a life it is. It is like an everyday person either trying to make a living or really make his life count.

Such ordinary people one day, through several series of resiliencies are able to discover, master and live an extra-ordinary and fulfilling life. Nobody wants to settle for the average, at least deep down in our souls. We have an essence that wants to live and love and matter.

I came across the story of one visionary called Joe Vitale. He typically tells us his 'ordinary' story that through resilience has now been converted into an 'extra-ordinary story'. A story that he was embarrassed to tell is now circulating the whole wide world. It is a story of a man who was once stuck, yet got out of it so gloriously that he is an inspiration to millions across the globe.

> *"The only cure of a painful past is the vision of your future"*
> —Mike Murdock

Before we can share the story, we need to look at the anatomy of being stuck. First off, let us mention that being stuck happens to everyone. *All that varies is the degree or the magnitude of the situation.* We should know that the anatomy of being stuck is a constant just like the constant pull of gravity along the earth's surface.

However, our look at being unstuck restricts itself to an assumption that the environment around which we live is conducive for success. In areas where there are man-made disasters such as war and ethnic cleansing, multitudes can be easily categorized as stuck. They have no freedom to work on their success; all they are doing is to survive, mostly escaping death.

One such a person is the now famous war child, Emmanuel Jal. Born in the war ravaged Southern Sudan, Emmanuel knew and participated in war as a child until later on he was rescued by a compassionate woman, who herself died few years later on. Jal tells of hardship like no one else I have heard speak about. He speaks of how starved they were to the degree that the flesh of fellow man seemed so gloriously succulent and edible. In fact, some soldiers would force their colleagues to urinate in a container and they would eat that urine. This act of desperation would haunt many soldiers in their minds and in the end, cause them to commit suicide.

> "Notice however that even in the darkest of moments, human beings have been accorded a strong measure of resilience. Both in manmade disasters and natural disasters, human beings have stories littered all over history of bounce and resilience. Most of these stories inspire us to be all we can be."

Yet Emmanuel Jal is one leading light that has come out of that man-made disaster as a gifted recording artists and peace ambassador, sharing his stories of encouragement across the world.

In situations where there are natural disasters such as fires, droughts, floods and tsunamis, individuals can get stuck if these situations are sustained over time.

Still, we have heard of great and resounding stories of resilience despite man-made and natural disasters.

The Holocaust was a man-made disaster whose sole goal was to systematically and ultimately decimate an entire race of people. Victor Frankl is a survivor of that despicable atrocity. He says that man can take from you everything he wants, but he will never take from you the power to make a choice of whether to be happy or sad. His is a signature story of resilience.

Slavery was another man-made disaster. Africans were systematically yanked from their native homes and shipped into foreign lands for slavery. Stories abound of scores who were dumped into the oceans by their captors who did not want to be caught in the act. The story of slavery especially in America took decades of resilience to turn around.

With slavery came heinous racial segregation that was institutionalized. Yet as dark as the age of racial segregation was, brilliant lights in the names of Rosa Parks and Martin Luther King Jr. are mentioned as signature stories of resilience. In the 1960's nobody in America would even imagine that that nation would have a black President. In 2008, it happened and in 2012 Barack Obama was re-elected as President of the United States…against all odds.

Apartheid in South Africa was a man-made disaster. It encroached on the freedom of Blacks in South Africa. As a result, it was easy for most blacks to get stuck as far as their ambitions in life were concerned. Yet as that went along, one man was locked away for agitating for the whole Black Nation to be unstuck. After 27 years, Nelson Mandela came out of prison and became the first Black President of South Africa, ruled for one term and handed over power. He is internationally respected to such an extent that every big name in this lifetime has an ambition to shake his hands. That is pure resilience.

Colonialism was a man-made phenomenon. In colonized nations, the natives were deprived of the necessary freedom to live, love and matter. In such conditions, it would be very easy to categorize their situation as stuck.

Taking a look at some of these situations helps us to put the aspect of being stuck into sharp perspective. We are not anticipating any man-made disasters, and as such we will be assuming that the pursuits of every human soul are done in a conducive human rights environment that accords every dreamer an opportunity to pursue their dreams to fulfillment.

> *"In the context of this book, being stuck refers to a state that is physical, mental, emotional or their compound that spells an illusionary dead end to one's pursuits in meeting a need, a want, a known vision or a true heart's desire".*

Notice however that even in the darkest of moments, human beings have been accorded a strong measure of resilience. Both in man-made and natural disasters, history is littered with stories of resilience. These stories inspire us to be all we can be.

Having said that, let us answer this important question:

**What does it mean to be stuck?**
In the context of this book, being stuck refers to a state that is physical, mental, emotional or their compound that spells an illusionary dead end to one's pursuits in meeting needs, wants, known vision or a true heart's desires. When this happens, an individual is deemed to be in a life crisis.

In other words, it is snapshot in a cross section of one's life in a moment in time. It is part and parcel of life. It is the color that makes our humanity real. It is the stuff that makes our stories of heroism believable. *It is a temporary situation.* Actually, a stuck situation is purposely designed to be temporary. The duration of time we take in our setback situations totally are dependent on *external factors* as well as *internal* or *personal factors*. The latter is much more powerful than the former.

It is thoroughly important to repeat what H. G. Wells said,

> *"What on earth would man do with himself if something didn't stand in the way?"*

Notice that the crisis is nothing but an *illusionary* dead end. In other words, to the unaccustomed, when a stuck situation shows up, they will react in such a way as to suggest that *there are no options* whatsoever, at least on their part, to get out.

It is this myth that I would like to exterminate in this book. Using our story, we will spend some time looking at Ben who got stuck severally, what he did, how he should have reacted and what lessons we must learn from him in order to build massive resilience in our lives.

Here is a wise saying that is worth noting. In fact, if there is any one thing that we should take home from the whole of these pages, it is this:

*Stuck situations are our biggest friends, our biggest catalyst for deep-seated essence unearthing personal revival and resilience. Stuck situations should be cherished when they show up!*

You will most definitely need the necessary skills and disposition to make sure that you harness all there is to harness in a stuck situation, and that is what we will be covering in these pages as we examine Ben's checkered career life.

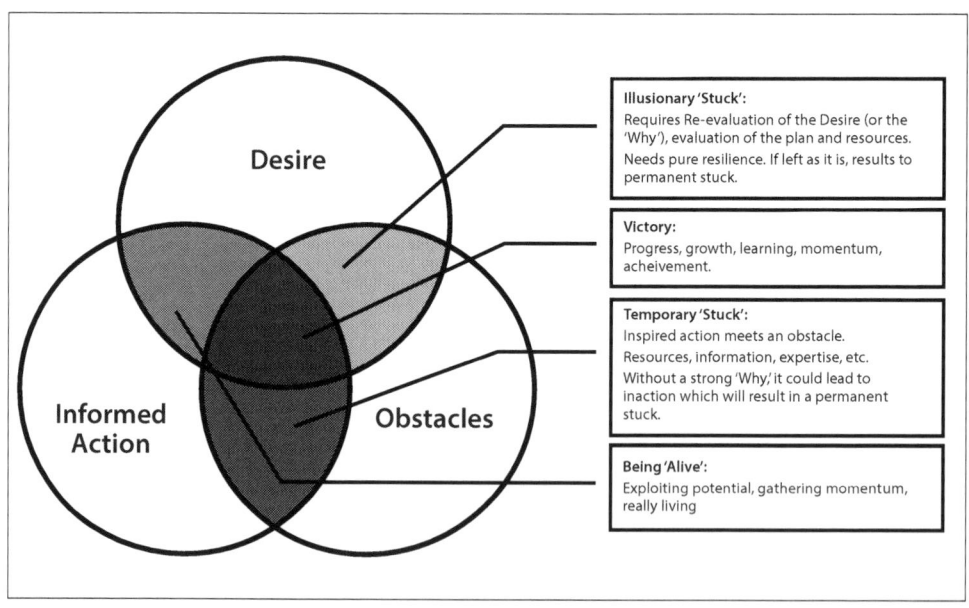

# WHAT CAUSES PEOPLE TO GET STUCK?

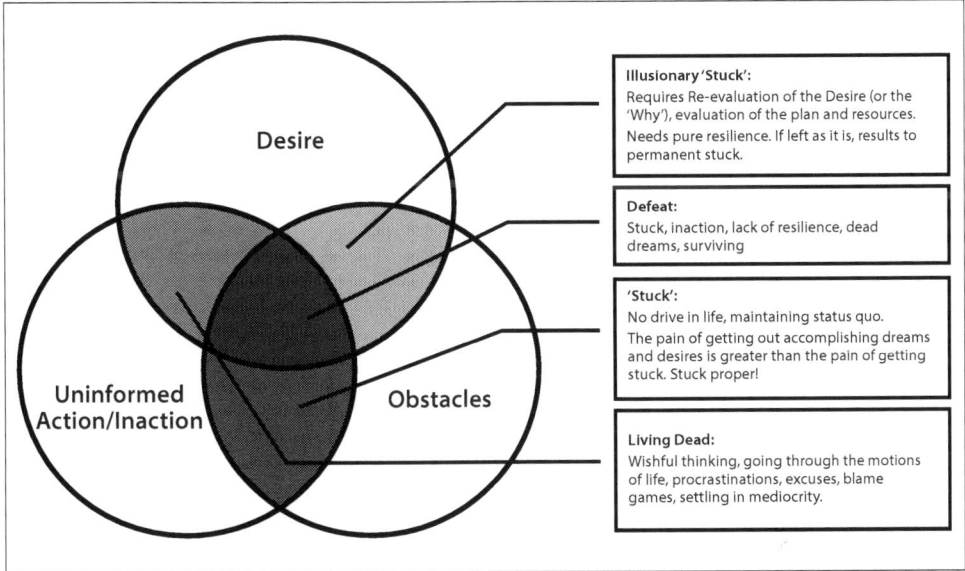

## THE FOLLOWING IS THE ANATOMY OF A STUCK STATE:

### 1. Desire:

The paradox of being stuck is found in taking action. Taking action is deeply rooted in having deep seated desire. All human beings have desires. The major reason as to why we pursue our desires is so that we can attain good feelings. In fact knowing one's true heart's desire is critical in understanding our stuck situations and orchestrating a bounce-back, or resilience.

Yet the word desire can take very many forms and shapes. It is a wide and general word that would encompass the following elements:

### Vision:

The clearer the vision is to an individual, the more resilient they tend to be when faced with obstacles. The people who have 'downloaded' and refined their vision create in them a strong 'why-power' that propels them against all odds.

On the same token, there would be individuals who are not so clear on what they really want in life. This forms the vast majority of people. The converse is also true. Those who are not clear on their personal vision or purpose in life tend to be in a perpetual stuck state. It is only when the light of their greatness is illuminated that they rise up above the level of mediocrity from the stuck position.

> *"Where there is no vision, the people perish"*
> —God

People who have no vision tend to 'settle'. Over time it becomes okay for them to go through life doing the bare minimum—putting food on the table and clothes on their backs. This is the worst form of stuck and it is common the world over. It is estimated that over 83% of the human population exist in this bracket.

**Needs:**
Everybody has these, starting from the unborn child to the eldest in society. The most basic needs are food, shelter and clothing. Other human needs include love, acceptance, safety and security. Every single individual looks out for these needs on a daily basis. A continued lack of any one of them can easily characterize a stuck situation. In the first chapter we summarized it by saying that stuck states are common to mankind…and you can see why.

**Wants:**
These go a little softer than the needs. We can do without some of the long lists of wants that we have. Wants basically gravitate towards what makes our living comfortable, easy, classy, exquisite and fast. It is interesting to note that as we move on in advancement, some of the things that would be included in the wants list are now easily finding space in our needs lists. Up until the 1990s we lived without cell phones. Today, this powerful, hand-held communication device is becoming a paramount item of our needs list.

As you can see, desire automatically sets up opportunities to be stuck. Any human being who lacks this component is not really living.

## 2. Action:
Paradoxically, it is inspired actions that lead to 'stuck'. At the center of a stuck situation, there is this illusion that there are no options to take. This comes up after one has taken action towards meeting a particular desire. This illusion mostly makes people to do nothing and resign in frustration.

> *"An important concept that successful people understand is that you are never stuck. You just keep re-creating the same experience over and over by thinking the same thoughts, maintaining the same beliefs, speaking the same words, and doing the same things"*
> –Jack Canefield, Author 'The Success Principles'

## 3. Obstacles:
Of course there are several things in play in this phase of the stuck state:

### Fear:
There is fear and then there is the fear of being afraid. These two things are extremely powerful forces that can condemn someone in a stuck situation for long. Fear paralyses people to inaction. Fear can also communicate to us that we are incapable of handling things. Yet the fear can be a very good friend. Bill Gates said the following:

> *"In business, by the time you realize that you are in trouble, it's too late to save yourself. Unless you are running scared all the time, you are gone!"*

Therefore, fear is a double edged sword: It both makes people to stay on track if well harnessed, but it also makes people stuck on their tracks if fully obeyed..

### Lack:
Probably, the biggest reason why many people stay in a crisis for long is the valid point of lacking things. The fact that I am lacking something does not necessarily mean that that thing does not exist. Many people stop in their tracks when it gets to their attention that they do not have something. Some will abandon projects, some will give up altogether, and some will even think they made the wrong decision in the first place to get started.

A state of lack for the most part reinforces the scarcity mentality that when it gets to someone, they feel inferior. However, provision was never a guarantee all the time. Also, when we are lacking in something, it does not mean that it does not exist in the world. It is in there somewhere. It is up to us to go get it. This of course means paying a certain price in exchange. Lack can be categorized as follows:

- **Resources:** Mostly this refers to money. Money can answer very many questions posed by lack. However, that being as it is, lack of money is not the greatest lack. There have been people with money who lost it in a short period of time because they lacked other things discussed below.
- **Mentors:** How many experiments did Edison do to invent the light? 1,000? I think so. Still, if he did not show his breakthrough to someone else, it might have taken more than those 1,000 attempts to get his breakthrough. My point is that it took 1,000 attempts for Edison, but subsequently, it takes just one attempt.
- Mentors are seasoned professionals who have been there and done that. They have also helped countless other people and thereby accumulated

years in experience. Without mentors, it is easy to wallow in a crisis for quite a while.
- **Teams:** We need as much help that we can get. That is why people get employed in the first place. There are two golden rules with forming a team: First, get the right positions. Second, fill those positions only with the right people! If you break one of these rules, you stay stuck in a crisis that would have otherwise not existed.
- **Ideas/Options:** Probably, the greatest lack that people have the world over is this one. That is why money is never the greatest lack… ideas are. If you were to be offered USD 10,000 today with the challenge that you produce all bullet point plan how to invest (not spend it) in five minutes…would you win that cash?
- A vast majority of people are stuck because of this point alone. They never have sat down to generate plans, goals, ideas and options to work with. Most people have one option: Get an office job after school. It is a good option…but honestly, it is NOT the only option. In fact, most people who do not have jobs categorize themselves as being stuck. Nothing could be further from the truth!
- **Knowledge:** "My people perish for lack of knowledge". When God says this, it tells you that it is not up to him for us to get the necessary knowledge. It is up to us. Lack of knowledge has always been widely advocated to be the reason for crisis in life. This is true. That is why Education is key in every government. However, it is the correct knowledge that will get me out of my hardship, not just academic knowledge. Academic knowledge is foundational, but not all sufficient.

### Feelings of unworthiness:

When Ben received the news about the company's contract, he knew that all was not well. It was a wake-up call for him to do something about it. However, Ben could not just take action. As he grew up, Ben was consummately passionate about studying and he really wanted to earn a University Degree. Part of this was the attention that his parents, especially his dad gave to this.

When Ben graduated from primary school top of his class, his dad was so proud of him, ecstatic to be exact. When Ben failed to get the cut-off points to join University, his dad was disappointed.

Consequently, Ben felt so unworthy for the most part. He would only rise to the fore of a group after a while of sitting down and assessing. In the case of the threat of a job loss, Ben did not start looking for another one because he was afraid he would not get one. This was because he felt unworthy. Many people are in this bracket. As long as they feel unworthy, they take no action. Yet taking action is imperative for them to navigate out of a crisis.

### Mental Conditioning:
People would or would not do things largely depending on their beliefs. Mental conditioning takes place in two ways: Either consciously or unconsciously. Sometimes, these two ways work at the same time. If we believe that we cannot do something, even if we do have the ability to do it, we will not take action!

In other words, our mental conditioning is much more powerful than our abilities. In fact, there are some people who believed that they could do something yet did not have the ability to do it…but astounded themselves by taking action.

Mental conditioning can happen in one of two ways:

- A devastating experience accompanied by words: Les Brown in his book *'Live your Dreams'* talks about the 'chicken man'. This man walks around pushing a shopping cart and making some chicken sounds. What happened is that once a family man in a perfect home, a fire gutted down his house and killed his young kids. His uncle upon arriving in the scene sharply rebuked him for not rescuing the kids and only rescuing himself, calling him…'Chicken'.
- The same words spoken over and over either by one person or by many people. A former boss of mine used to say that if you woke up one morning feeling fine and someone told you that you look bad and you need to see a doctor, you would not give them a thought. If a second person tells you the same thing, you might laugh at the conspiracy. But if all that continues and the fifth person that same day gave you that feedback, you would definitely go see a doctor even if you felt fine!

### Hope:
This is one of the most detrimental philosophies that cause people to get stuck. We discuss it fully in Chapter 4

**4. Inaction:**
Herein is the acceleration of a stuck situation. Inaction directly leads to a stuck situation more often than not. The main reason as to why people seldom take action when faced with obstacles is a paralysis caused mainly by fear. No, it is not the fear of taking action, but rather, it is the fear of the manifestation of what they do not want to see happen as a result of facing the obstacles.

---

*"Hope is the dark side of positive thinking—it doesn't require any action*

> *and rarely results in the desired outcome. People who hope expect something without working for it and get upset when someone else receives something they deserved"*
> ~ Kim George

People are afraid of the stuck state that they wish it was not a reality. The paradox as we have seen is that no one is exempt from being stuck. A resilient mind will at the earliest opportunity make the necessary mental adjustments, accept and even craft the possible Worst Case Scenario and start operating from that angle.

> *"Work brings profit, but mere talk leads to poverty"*
> —Proverbs 14:23

Inaction is also brought about by the illusion that there are no options. For the most part, as much as people do not like being in the uncomfortable stuck situation, they tend to seek emotional refuge away from it. They tend to seek something that can pacify the situation. They tend to free their scared and battered souls from the immense pressure that the stuck situation comes with.

That is why many people do not stop to think that the way out of the stuck is to ride it out. Most people concentrate on looking outside of themselves to find a way out. This effectively transfers the responsibility of working the situation out to someone else…and for the most part to time elapsing so that the situation remedies itself.

Inaction is commonly referred to as 'waiting'.

> *"Waiting can be a philosophy which causes adaptation to your present and then destroys your future"*
> —Mike Murdock

Inaction is also laced with 'hoping'. The combination of waiting and hoping are sometimes the foundation of disillusionment. It is easy to see that for the most part, where there is hope, the person in a stuck situation waits. The fulfillment of a hoped situation is always in the hands of the divine. That however should not emasculate an individual from taking action with what they have at hand. Taking action now is constituent of being brave enough to face the worst case scenario here and now other than waiting and hoping for things to change. A search on Wikipedia for James Stockdale, Prisoner of war in Vietnam reveals a very interesting rendition of his story by Author Jim

Collins, Good to Great:

> In a business book by James C. Collins called 'Good to Great', Collins writes about a conversation he had with Stockdale regarding his coping strategy during his period in the Vietnamese POW camp.
>
> "I never lost faith in the end of the story, I never doubted not only that I would get out, but also that I would prevail in the end and turn the experience into the defining event of my life, which, in retrospect, I would not trade'.
>
> When Collins asked who didn't make it out of Vietnam, Stockdale replied:
>
> "Oh, that's easy, the optimists. Oh, they were the ones who said, 'We're going to be out by Christmas.' And Christmas would come, and Christmas would go. Then they'd say, 'We're going to be out by Easter.' And Easter would come, and Easter would go. And then Thanksgiving, and then it would be Christmas again. And they died of a broken heart."
>
> Stockdale then added:
>
> This is a very important lesson. You must never confuse faith that you will prevail in the end—which you can never afford to lose—with the discipline to confront the most brutal facts of your current reality, whatever they might be." –**Wikipedia Search of James Stockdale, Prisoner of War in Vietnam**

Ben was a grand master at waiting. He was good at not only hoping but also giving hope. Those two things have their place yet in Ben's several stuck situations, those two are the main culprits. It goes without saying that the same applies to as many as 80% of the human population.

One more derivative of waiting is normally fueled by a promise given on an action taken. We will look at how Ben wasted a whole two years because of operating on a promise in the coming chapters. We will learn what Ben did and how he at the end of the day totally annihilated the object of the promise in order to start afresh. With the promise out of sight, Ben had the power back in his hands to do something…anything that would propel him towards his desires.

The error of hoping is the main culprit for inaction which leads to being disillusioned and ultimately being stuck.

Waiting is not doing nothing. Waiting without action is the recipe of disillusionment. Waiting is a massive force not a suspension of living.

> "Once you decide in your mind that you cannot do it, that's just it. We could fly in professors from across the globe but they would not change anything".

> *"Waiting is often a demonic strategy"*
> —Mike Murdock

There is a heaven and earth difference between waiting while doing nothing and submitting to a process. When planted, seeds go through a germination process to sprout. That is a sure documented process, as much as a farmer doesn't have an active hand in it. A baby in the womb is not stuck, it's in the process. A vision not put to process however, is stuck for sure.

**Remember the law of entropy:**

"Any organized process naturally tends to decline to a chaotic state if we leave it alone"

In latter chapters, we will discuss how we can leverage on stuck situations by changing our understanding on waiting for processes to mature.

**Settling and Giving up:**

> *"The brick walls are there for a reason. The brick walls are not there to keep us out. The brick walls are there to give us a chance to show how badly we want something. Because the brick walls are there to stop the people who don't want it badly enough. They're there to stop the other people."*
> – Randy Pausch

The greatest aspiration for young adults is to 'settle down'. It is one of their biggest dreams whose ultimate goal is comfort. Settling down is an illusion. It really is. The moment people settle down, they start losing impact. Humans have been made in such a way that we are always goal seeking. The greatest disadvantage that human beings have is that they do not know all the fine details about what they do desire at one point in time.

Things are always opening up to us every single day. The more we draw near to something, the greater clarity we get. The greater the increase of ideas we get when we keep pursuing our goals. Therefore, settling down is an illusion. It just never happens!

Giving up on the other hand starts with an internal mental assent. It is easy to give up when all around us seems to be impossible and against us. When all the efforts we are putting out are not producing any tangible result in the present, we just resign to the thought that "it's no use". If that state continues, it becomes a belief. Beliefs are very strong centers of success or failure. It is Harrison Ford I believe who said, "If you think you can and if you think you can't, either way you got it right".

The anatomy of giving up is steeped either in measuring results of our action against a seeming impossibility or by just looking at the seeming impossibility and counting our present resources unable to solve it. In other words, we give it a try and if we see no tangible change, we conclude that our actions can't help. Or we just look at the enormity of the situation and dare not even try. We are in need of both persistence and determination.

> *"Not until the pain of the same is greater than the pain of change will you embrace change."*
> —Dave Ramsey: American financial author and nationally syndicated radio host

Let us remind ourselves of this quote:

> *"What on earth would man do with himself if something didn't stand in the way?"*
> —H.G. Wells

Our perception of trouble will determine whether we will be stuck or we will thrive. As soon as a life is conceived, trouble is an appointment. We need to understand that that is the way this world is structured.

> *"Man is born to trouble as sure as sparks fly upwards"*
> –Job in the Bible

When planted, a seed has to break out of its hard outer shell to germinate. Even then, it has to break out of the ground that covers it. Without pressure, life looses structure, meaning and form. The paradox is that the human body loves so much comfort. The human mind loves not to be disturbed. Yet for progress, there must be obstacles. Success in my definition is the continual mastery of challenges.

I remember Peter J Daniels speaking of an encounter that he and Norman Vincent Peale had one day. As they were walking down the road, they met a man who recognized Dr. Norman Vincent Peale. This man was so excited and the encounter went something like this:

**Stranger:** My God, This must be my lucky day, are you Dr. Norman Vincent Peale?
**Norman:** Yes I am
**Stranger:** Are you the author of 'The Power of Positive Thinking', a book that has sold millions and been translated to several languages? Are you the one?

**Norman:** Yes I am. I am a minister of the Gospel....what can I do to help you?
**Stranger:** Well this certainly is my lucky day, because I need your help. I have all these problems that keep following me...can you help me get rid of them?
**Norman:** Well, as a minister of the gospel, I have just left a group of 1500 people back there who have no problem at all. Would you like me to take you to them?
**Stranger:** Yes Sir, I need to meet them and talk to them.
**Norman:** Well, they are in the cemetery!

Every human life must face obstacles to be beautiful. It is cliché about a butterfly being helped out of a cocoon. Without the pressure of its 'birth', the wings become weak and the creature dies in minutes.

One of the biggest concepts of this book is that our *fundamental nature* is shaped in the moments of pressure. When Ben's brother Tim died, Ben went through a tumult of emotions. No doubt that experience shaped his young life one way or another. When he walked out of his first job in the hope that he would be successful in the interview he attended, having lost chance, he faced tremendous pressure that no doubt shaped his life. He would not be the same humble boy if he had not gone through it.

---

> *"Problems are opportunities for significance. Without a problem, you do not have a future. Problems create necessity"*
> —Mike Murdock

---

We all know about inoculations and vaccines. In order to vaccinate against polio for example, the vaccine contains the polio virus in it. That is why great achievers who are resilient have the stuck virus in them. That is why they see obstacles as opportunities.

To the unschooled in life, obstacles must be avoided at all costs. In fact, as a natural instinct, we all want to shun obstacles like a plague! I have seldom seen one who moved closer to his essence in life when all was well. It is almost always while all hell was breaking loose.

It is in those moments of pressure that a soul is forced to ask the right questions about life. In life, questions are answers. Such soul searching questions always have answers, you can bet on it.

However, when all is well, the bread is buttered and there is minimal pressure on a soul, especially one that does not know their essence in life, these questions are seldom asked. The real meaning of life is to matter beyond scheduled success...and to make a difference in the lives of others. The *meaning of life* is to be more of ourselves that we were intended to be on an ever increasing measure.

This *life purpose* is mostly unlocked through bravely facing challenges, obstacles, problems, disappointments and general stuck situations. The quality of a problem solver is how many challenges they have put under…and how many victories are under their belts.

The measure of a professional is the degree of resilience that they have built over time. The faster one bounces back after a fall, the faster they build their resilience.

> *"One of the major ways of life helping us focus on what really matters is to throw us challenges.*
>
> *The challenges are not just to be solved, but individuals are supposed to grow with the mastering of these challenges. As much as success is a continuous mastery of challenges, the real meaning of life is of a higher gravity than just attaining success".*

*"The measure of success is not whether you have a tough problem to deal with, but whether it's the same problem you had last year"*
—John Foster Dulles

Here is the thing: We can circumvent obstacles, solve them or do nothing about them and stay in a stuck state. Those three are the only choices we have. The wise and resilient will want to continually solve problems.

## The following is Joe Vitale's story:

> I knew I wanted to be an author when I was a teenager. I wanted to write books and plays that made people happy. Everywhere I looked I saw unhappy people. I believed I could help them with humor and stories. During that time of the mid-1970s, I watched sports. I don't today, but back then the Dallas Cowboys were the rage. Roger Staubach and Tom Landry were heroes. I got caught up in the excitement and felt the place for me to make my name was in Dallas, Texas.
>
> I lived in Ohio at the time. Born and raised there. I worked on the railroad as a trackman, doing heavy labor all day long, working weekends and summers since the age of five.
>
> I saved my money, packed up my bag, and took a bus to Dallas. It took three days to get there. I was lost in the big city, of course. Being born in a small town in Ohio didn't prep me for the hustle and bustle of a city the size of Dallas.
>
> Before long, I wanted out. But I still wanted to be an author. At that time major companies were building oil and gas pipelines in Alaska and the Middle East, and offering to pay big bucks if you were willing to go to either place.
>
> I wasn't keen on going to a foreign country and doing more labor, but I saw a chance to

make money, save it, and then go on a sabbatical where I could write for a few months or even a year.

It seemed like a brilliant strategy.

I answered one of the newspaper ads that promised to get me pipeline work at an extraordinary hourly wage. I went in their office, met an upbeat salesperson, and ended up giving him all of my money - my entire savings, about a thousand dollars at the time - based on his promise that I'd have overseas pipeline work in a week or two.

You might guess part of what happened next - but you won't guess all of it. Within a week or so, the company that took all of my money went out of business. Their doors were closed, no one answered the phone, and no forwarding addresses could be found. Shortly after that, the company went bankrupt.

And not long after that, the owner of the company committed suicide.

There was no one left to try to get my money back from. I was alone. I was broke. I was in Dallas, far from home.

I confess that my ego got in the way here. My family back in Ohio would have taken me back in and welcomed me back home. But I was headstrong and determined to somehow survive.

Well, I did survive - by sleeping in church pews, on the steps of a post office, in a bus station. It wasn't an easy time, as you can imagine, and I never used to talk about it. It was too embarrassing. When I told this story at dinner, everyone agreed I had to share it with you.

They said that people are finding themselves in the same situation - they trusted a government, or a corporation, or a person, or a bank, and now they are losing their homes and their jobs.

Hearing that I went through the same thing three decades ago and not only survived but prospered to a level that the Joe Vitale of 30 years ago could hardly imagine, ought to be inspiring to you, too.

I got off the streets and out of poverty by constantly working on myself - reading self-help books, taking action, scrambling at times by taking whatever work I could find, but always — always, ALWAYS focusing on my vision: to one day be an author of books and audio programs that would come from the ideas in those books that help people be happy and stay inspired.

If you're in a place right now that doesn't feel so good or seem too safe, I urge you to remind yourself that this is only temporary. This is the cure for despair.

As I heard someone say not too long ago, "The downtimes only last for a season; the grass will grow again".

This is simply current reality, and current reality can change. You can help it along by doing what you know and need to do. But remember, the sun will shine again. It always does.

Your job right now is to focus on what you want and keep it in sight. Yes, keep taking action; yes, stay positive and surround yourself with positive people; yes, be of support to others.

But, remember, if I or anyone else can survive homelessness, poverty, job loss, or any other hard time, then you can survive it, too. Please hang in there.

One last thing: I admit that there were times I wanted to throw in the towel and get myself out of this life. Thank God, I stuck around. Had I left early, I would have missed a life of magic and wonder, success and fame I never dreamed of before, priceless relationships and experiences, and more.

I have no idea what wonderful *good* is headed your way - and neither do you.

What you have to do is stay the course and follow your heart.

—Joe Vitale, ADVANTEDGE NEWSLETTER, "The Cure of Despair" January 2013

## CHAPTER 3:
# "Unless Those Days Are Shortened…"

*"Sometimes when things fall apart, they might actually be falling right into place"*

**-Quote**

Someone said that you never know how strong you are up until the time that being strong is the only option that is available. That is true. Yet in the being strong, there is always is a timeframe of endurance that we can handle it. If the situation pervades for longer time, it might break us. Much like a potter knows exactly what time to pull the vessel from the furnace, if he delays one minute, his artifact will be destroyed by the fire.

As much as we will see how 'shortcuts' are dangerous, I know that there is no human being on the face of the earth who would not invite the chance to 'shorten' his days of being in a crisis or experiencing a setback. In fact we all want to get out of hardship the very moment it knocks on our door! That is our natural response in close to 100% of all the adversities that we face. The good news however is that those days can be shortened…both virtually and literally. We know from human experience that some hardships can take one month yet it would seem that we were stuck for a whole year. In this chapter, we will learn to erase that illusion that the setback is here forever and see how we can have those days shortened.

Ben was over 30 years old, yet had no vision, no purpose, no mission and no general direction in life. You see, when life is sizzling, such a focus on the essence of life is normally relegated to the periphery of existence.

The interesting thing in the whole circus is that a man relaxes and settles down in daily chores, he misses the urgency in finding his essence in life. Isn't it deceiving to think that you are finally engaged in life, go after these activities with reckless abandonment yet not knowing that [the activities] "they are not it?"

> *"A desk is a dangerous place from which to watch the world"*
> ——John Le Carre

And here is the Paradox: You have everything to do, yet in all the doing, nothing really counts in the end…technically. Why do I say technically? Well, it is because life has a marvelous way of balancing itself out. As such, even the mundane of activities we engage in for decades can never be counted as waste. As long as a soul rises up and embraces his or her essence, all the experiences whether good or bad that they have gone through become such beautiful and firm foundations to serve the rest of life. The design of life is such that fulfillment is derived from finding one's purpose and serving in it. This ought to be a deliberate process yet for the most part it is not. And herein lies the greatest tragedy in Ben's Century: great advancements in Technology and communication, infrastructure and governance, and yet Billions (with a B) on the face

> "The design of life is such that fulfillment is derived from finding one's purpose and serving in it. This ought to be a deliberate process yet for the most part it is not. And herein lies the greatest tragedy in Ben's Century: great advancements in Technology and communication, infrastructure and governance, and yet Billions (with a B) on the face of the earth are stuck not knowing their fundamental nature in life."

A little over two hours after they had embarked on their journey deeper into the interior of the country, Ben and his Team Leader arrived at their next major stop, where another field team personnel was waiting eagerly. The road was good enough. In Ben's assessment, there would be need for lots of work to be done for the product he was championing to take over.

Ben and his Team Leader were welcomed by Silas, the second field Personnel that he was meeting. Silas was older than Ben. He even had his own family. He was a humble man, extremely pliable…and sometimes mesmerized at Ben's presence. He took them to the nearest outlet where Ben and the Team Leader would inspect the condition of the market.

Things looked promising. Ben was ready to hit the road again and go deeper into the interior. The weather seemed as if it would allow some heavy rains later on in the evening. So Ben arranged to have a quick lunch before launching out. He had asked his Team Leader to arrange his itinerary in such a way that in two day's time, Ben would have covered the whole region and finally have a meeting with all the five members of that team.

Ben's heart was so full of advice to give to his team, his mind so full of knowledge that he would like his Team to grasp in the meeting. He looked forward to this meeting with great enthusiasm, although it was to happen in two days.

Unbeknown to Ben, he was homing in unconsciously on his essence in life. He talked with passion. There was this time that a temporary team he had hired to help iron out hiccups on the initial stages of the product launch got mesmerized. The client had a galore of complaints about the team and Ben was forced to act. He called this team back to the office for a hard talk. Well, it never really turned out to be a hard talk after all. It was an inspirational talk.

You could feel the care. You could feel the passion. You could feel the motivation.

So this team that showed up from the office thinking that their goose was cooked was back in the market doing wonders, being thoroughly motivated by Ben. Looking back at those times, Ben wonders where the inspiration and motivation came from.

> *The crowd, the world, and sometimes even the grave, step aside for the man who knows where he's going, but pushes the aimless drifter aside*
> ~Ancient Roman saying

Ben wonders how he easily anchored his phrases and used his personal stories to talk to this team. He had recently discovered Success Magazine and was devouring it at any opportunity. You do not read such a magazine and your conversation remains the same. So inherently, Ben changed and moved towards his passion. Unfortunately, this was unbeknownst to him.

So after a hurried lunch meal and final instructions to Silas, Ben and his navigator Team Leader hit the road again. His Team Leader had insisted that there was a certain region in the market that Ben must see. They now needed to use an all-weather road to get to this interesting and remote location.

**'Form One'**
Ben put on his inspirational songs through his phone, connecting one earpiece and leaving the other for conversation purposes with his team leader. For some reason, he was too cautious driving on this road, so much so that other vehicles overtook them easily.

He got so concerned that he decided to play 'catch up'. That is another major lesson in life. The environment in which we grow or work will most definitely determine our outcome. There are two types of environments. There are those that have been deliberately set up to inspire and motivate. The key word here is deliberate. Of course, there are also those environments that have been left by default to stay the way they ever were from the beginning. In the end, they do not inspire but set up a vicious cycle of rituals without meaning.

Remember the competition that Ben was exposed to in his primary school? Well, that played a whole lot in shaping and sharpening him. Yet more was yet to come. In 1993, Ben was the first form one to report to school. Partly because his parents were so happy and so eager to see him admitted on one of the most prestigious schools in the province. That was wrong according to the un-written code of being 'cool' in school. You don't just come on the first day... you bid your time.

I have to tell you that that dreaded thing called bullying that form ones go through happened to him. Ben thought and he still does that all bullies are miscreants... and he insists that he is not biased to say this. There are some who bullied him that are reading this... some are dead, others are whatever place they are in the world. Ben wonders how they would great each other today when they meet... few decades later.

**First time experiences**
Yet the experience of being a form one will always be one of those fundamental 'shapers' of Ben's life. To be honest with you, despite the negatives of bullying and all the discomforts that he faced there, he came to realize that he would gladly go back to that situation where he was a form one once again.

In fact, he would do that again and again and again as the chances come. You know why? 'Form ones' grow! Pretty soon they catch up with the culture at school. They get up to speed with the lingo... and smart ones can easily pretend to be 'form two' in less than a week!

Seriously, we have those form one situations all around us. You are newly married... guess what? You are a form one of sorts in that arena. You are about to grow. You are about to learn some new things. You had better... since growth is good for us.

There is no point for us being in 'form one' in theory... it is OK, but nothing replaces the tangible experience we gain when physically there.

You can read as much as you want (and Ben reads a lot by the way) but when you get that new job as a sales executive, guess what? 'Form One' once again! I think you get the point.

One thing that really gave him a culture shock in his first year of high-school and pretty much the rest of the four years he spent there was the stark realization that there were some guys that were way, and I mean way ahead of him 'upstairs'. Whereas from his rural school he came tops at the final exams, Ben found out that in his stream in 'form one', he was at best, 70th! Oh! How the mighty fall!

And that is a pretty good thing if you ask me. That is why our kids need to be exposed to as much competition as possible.

The same thing happened to him when Ben joined college. As much as he studied (and study he did... Ben remembers how fellow students would come to the library to specifically marvel 'how Ben is studying'), there was still people way ahead of him... and to them it came naturally.

Needless to say, as much as we love comfort, it is good to have 'form one' situations as often as possible, that way, we tend to grow.

So you could say that Ben was in a 'form One' situation once again even as he tried to play catch up with the rather accustomed drivers on this route. It would be fair to suggest that most of these drivers were in the same situation Ben finds himself now: green between the ears.

The first few minutes of catching up were OK. The car was well serviced. Ben realized that it was rather more comfortable to go faster on the rough road than to take each bump and pothole one at a time. Within some time, Ben had become so accustomed that he was enjoying the experience.

The very next thing that happened to Ben was another first! He had never ever in his life been in this situation. Apparently, the terrain he was on was rather slippery with many pebbles on the road in a nearly steep valley. Ben realized a little bit late that he needed to reduce the speed. That was a mistake. The car skidded and rolled over twice before hitting a bunker on the side of the road!

Amazingly, he was calm at heart. His mind started racing. He had watched many movies where cars exploded with the occupants inside during an accident. Ben also realized that at some instances, the very seat belts that are used to protect us from damaging our organs in accidents could very well be the traps for our death in a vehicle in an accident.

Thank God for seatbelts. Ben knows that if he had not insisted like he usually did to every occupant in his vehicle to fasten their seatbelts, this would have been fatal. Presently, Ben kicked the windshield of the car to break it. He managed to free himself from his seatbelt and that was a relief...a major one at that. The car engine still raced.

As fast as he could, Ben gets out of the vehicle onto the road and helped his team leader who was presently dazed, to get out. A certain elderly lady was at hand...she was taking care of a herd of cattle alongside the road. For some reason, she was not moved by this accident. She must have been used to such like sights. Ben got to learn later on that that spot was a dark spot on that road.

In fact the elderly lady had some kind of understanding with the local traffic police officers. She must have called them for they showed up approximately ten minutes after the accident.

Meanwhile, this man who was on a roll had received some 'strength' to go on. There is something unique that happens when you go through your worst and you come out alive. Ben swears to date that he felt so inspired that he honestly figured that the damage of the vehicle was not that much and that if there was a way he could just get it on its wheels and resume the journey!

His Team Leader was now in tears. What a sight! A grown up man weeping uncontrollably like a baby! The man was lamenting that he nearly died yet he did not have a child at that point in time! Oh! The focus of the masses! Come to think of it. What would be your greatest regret if you were to die today? If death came knocking all of a sudden…what would be the loose end that is untied that you would regret not to have attended to? Your answer is a clue of what matters in your life right now. For this Team Leader, it is about fathering a child!

The police officers came armed with their towing vehicles, took some information from a simple enquiry from Ben and the elderly lady. The vehicle was towed back to the nearest town where Ben and his Team Leader had left Silas. They checked into a simple clinic and were treated of minor wounds. Meanwhile, Ben's Team Leader still cried like a baby. It was all Ben could do to hug him and say a short prayer to encourage the man.

Anyway, Ben was so on fire that he decided then and there to summon the rest of the team members in that region for a meeting at his current location. He just could not see the planned meeting done away with. The members obliged. This did not go well with Ben's boss however. He thought that Ben and the Team Leader needed to be in hospital as soon as possible, not spending needless time in the field.

**Avoiding Re-inventing the wheel—the ultimate shortcut**
Ben was glad to have his meeting, although hurried. He never focused on the accident. We are talking about an accident that just happened less than twelve hours the previous day. Yet this man on fire was busy inspiring his Team. What he spoke that day was pure inspiration. Pure inspiration comes from a man who just faced death or serious injury but came out unscathed. Ben cannot remember another time in his life that he was so engaged like he was this time. His team members were most definitely mesmerized…and inspired.

Yet again, this was one of the most critical moments in Ben's life. You could say that Ben had his feet firmly on his 'acres of diamond'. But could he see that? Did he even notice it?

> *"Life can only be understood backwards, but it must be lived forwards"*
> —Soren Kierkegaard

Those are very pertinent questions. Let us leave them however to ask the following more important questions. *Is it possible that Ben would know his 'acres of diamond' earlier? Is it possible that he could know about his essence at school? Could this stuck executive know his calling at two years old?*

These questions need to be answered. In the view of people being stuck, we could also ask the following questions: *Is there a way that a life crisis can be done away with? Is there a way that those days of distress and despair could be shortened?* Am sure more than seven billion people would be interested in the answers to these two questions.

The answer is found in this statement: Questions are answers! For every question out there, there is an answer. And the answer to all these questions posed already is an emphatic YES!

A vast majority of people are still engaged in that folly or re-inventing the wheel. We have very many examples of people who have made it in life, yet we still struggle at least the same way they did. Granted, their struggles taught them invaluable lessons that we could also learn.

*When we talk about shortening the time, we are talking about doing all that is in our power to evade re-inventing the wheel.* Could Ben know some things in his life earlier? Yes he could. How? By references!

> *"How many joys are crushed underfoot because people look up at the sky and disregard what is at their feet?"*
> ~ Author Unknown

Short days are not just in length. It is true that with the references in place, the days of seeking one's essence can be shortened. It is also true that with the references, the days of staying stuck in one place can also be shortened. Yet even if they were long days in the illusion of time, they would be days of quality. They would be short since one already knows their essence. All they are doing is amassing all they can while in the crisis to help serve in their essence. All they are doing is building resilience and bounce. All they are doing is refining their fundamental nature, reaffirming it and being sharper.

So how exactly would Ben shorten his days of seeking his essence? There are four major methods that he could use.

## FIVE WAYS TO SHORTEN THE DAYS OF A CRISIS:

### 1. Deliberate Questions:
*The greatest disservice that human beings render to themselves is to settle.* People for the most part surrender to norms, rituals and tradition without questioning. They settle and accept life the way it is 'handed down' to them.

*"Maybe, God wanted me to be singe"*, a broken hearted lady would say. However life and the meaning of it is seldom found on the surface. That is why at birth, a child comes with an awesome sense of curiosity. It is this curiosity that helps them to learn new things. Unfortunately, the curiosity is normally leveled off with the environment and the general acceptance of the way things are run. A child who asks: *"Dad must I really go to school?"* is not to be seen as rude. That question posed must have an answer. For the most part, the child asking this question is labeled rebellious. How sad!

I am not just talking about questions for the sake of questions. I am talking about prodding questions that are deliberate in nature. *We will only experience our future to the degree of the deep questions that we not only ask but keep asking.* Questions are an invitation for opened doors… knowledge, and wisdom. Questions break a stalemate. You can actually ask your way directly out of a stuck situation.

The point to note here is that these questions have got to be deliberate. Ben needed and still does need to learn how to ask quality questions. Throughout all the incidents of life, it would be sad for us to miss the opportunities to ask the right questions.

When Ben finds himself in stuck situations, he can do one of two things: He can accept that this is what life is serving and with time it will all end…or he can choose to ask the relevant questions that will ultimately see him through.

The exercise of deliberately asking questions is not necessarily hinged on the questions themselves but on the reception of the answers. As much as it is important to learn to ask questions, it is equally important to learn how to anticipate answers and when they come, how to receive them. There is no question that does not have an answer.

The answers we get are our blue prints for action. It is important to take action, and it is important to take informed action. In his book, 'The Answer to How is Yes' Peter Block insists that the correct question to ask is not How. This question should only be asked when the fundamental nature of life has been identified. When we know the why of the How…then we can ask the how. When we take action on the answers that come, we find that we have generated just about enough passion to see us through. Peter Block says the following:

> *"It always struck me that that I can write or speak the most radical thoughts imaginable. I can advocate revolution, the end of leadership, the abolition of appraising each other, the empowerment of the least among us, the end of life on the planet as we know it, and no one ever argues with me. The only questions I hear are "How do you get there from here? Where has this worked? What would it cost and what is the return on investment?"*
> *This has led me to the belief that the questions about How? are more interesting than any answer to them might be. They stand for some deeper concerns. So in this book, the starting point is to question the questions."*
> –Peter Block, The Answer to How? is Yes, Page 2

This makes a lot of sense to me. It talks about the levels of questions that we can have. The longer we ask, the deeper we get. The more we stay in the asking mode, the closer we get to essence answers.

> *There is depth in the question "How do I do this"? that is worth exploring. The question is a defense against the action. It is a leap past the question of purpose, past the question of intentions, and past the drama of responsibility. The question "How?"—more than any other question— looks for the answer outside of us. It is an indirect expression of our doubts.*
> *…"Choosing Freedom, Service, and Adventure"*
> —Peter Block, Stewardship, (p. 234)

Remember that a question is a door and all success is determined by questions. Dr. Mike Murdock says:

> *"Answers can hide from anything but questions. Wisdom can hide from anything but questions."*

Now, we also need to learn how we can ask empowering questions. There is a difference between empowering questions and disempowering questions. A question such as *"Why am I not a good enough parent"* for example dis-empowers you. A much better question would be *"What action do I need to take so I can be the most joyous parent on earth?"* Such a question generates options rather than close them down as the former question does.

## 2. Mentors:

*"The purpose of mentorship is to help someone you love avoid pain"*, says Dr. Mike Murdock. Here is the thing though: mentors do not choose us, we choose them. If a stuck executive would have his time in obscurity shortened, it is of necessity that he should have mentors and coaches around his life. A high performing Director of a company normally answers to a board. This board keeps him under enough pressure to perform. Without this board, it is pretty much easy to become complacent. Without mentors and coaches, or people that we are accountable to, it is possible that we can stay in a stuck environment longer than we should.

Mentors have already gone ahead and probably experienced even worse forms of being stuck. They are in a pole position to give directions. I heard Dr. Mike Murdock talk of a 20 year old girl that he gave an assignment to do… she was not to go back to him until she had 25 questions answered. When she followed through, she went back to this mentor with US $ 100,000 that a particular company owed him! I am sure that that was not all that the girl gained. She must have gained a wealth of experience in negotiations, sales, patience and presentation.

The question that we most probably need to ask ourselves is this: Who are our mentors? This question must remain valid whether or not we are in a stuck situation.

Harvey Mackay is the New York Times Number 1 Best Selling Author of several books, including *'Swimming with the Sharks'*. This man of tremendous influence in the Sales arena says the following about Mentors:

I personally believe that one of the cancers of our generation is the lack of mentors/coaches. They have all been fired…or were never hired in the first place. You might be shocked at how easy it would be to become a protégé. Many people would want to listen to a Billionaire explain how they made their first Million. In this technology world, it is very easy for me to be Dr. Mike Murdock's protégé, Peter J Daniels' protégé, and so on. Mentors help us get to the other side of our stuck situation faster.

Here is the thing though: We do not amass mentors just for the sake of it. The real gist of having a mentor is taking incessant action on what they require us to. Believe me, they know better. It is my mentor Dr. Mike Murdock who said, *"Young people trust, mature people test"*. Enough said.

Mentorship is learning from someone else's losses. This means that you do not need to incur the same losses that someone else did...now, I am not talking of using mentorship to totally avoid being stuck. Being stuck is one of the major blessings life can ever afford you. However, remaining stuck is one of the most bizarre things you can go through. A mentor knows exactly what to do and what not to do in order to get out of a stuck situation. He or she has been there and done it. The shortcut out of a stuck situation is through mentorship, Period!

> *"I've had 20 coaches, if you can believe it. And that's not a typo. I have a speech coach, I have a writing coach, I have a humor coach, I've got a language coach, and on and on".*

I believe one of the greatest killers of our people in the present age is silence. People, especially in hardship do not want to talk. This is partly because we always have this idea of putting our best foot forward, and now sadly, we cannot do so in our hardship. We want to 'resurface' when we are driving and having loads of cash to show. When stuck, we tend to hibernate. It is a strange strategy that keeps people locked in an adversity longer than they should. People need to talk, confide, be vulnerable and share candidly about their fears as well as their aspirations. Just one conversation with a fellow human being who understands is able to literally inject life back into your soul...like mouth to mouth resuscitation. As you learn to talk to people, remember to balance: Do not just talk about your woes and worries, talk also about your greatest desires, visions and aspirations.

**3. Books/References:**
It is commonly said that successful people have large libraries while most unsuccessful people have large TV sets. I could not agree more. Someone else said that TV is chewing gum for the eyes. Granted, chewing gum does something to your mind...but TV for the most part entertains more than it educates. A book like **Think and Grow Rich** took more than a decade in preparation, research and writing. That Book is a condensation of several concepts of success from big time visionaries. Again, people would pay top dollar to go listen to a Billionaire instruct them how to make a Billion. Gladly, such information is as common as table salt these days.

If a stuck executive would want to shorten the days of the 'stuck', he would do well not only to read as many books as possible, but also to apply the knowledge and the nuggets gained. Books are shortcuts to mentors. Most of modern day mentors have published books about their successes. In fact, it can be said that some mentors mentor us through the books, periodicals and articles that they churn out on a consistent basis.

The worst thing you can see is a stuck executive having no plan about his mind. It is a sad statistic that many people spend most of their valuable finances on clothes than they do on books. Peter J Daniels is an Australian Billionaire who at 70- plus years of age still trots the globe (2014) sharing his information in Seminars, Conferences and Church Services. Yet Peter was never formally educated. Peter J Daniels took upon himself to educate himself through reading books on History and Economics. He can now give advice to anybody about great topics like Starting a Business, Sales, Entrepreneurship, Banking and Finance. He did this solely through the self Education that he took himself through.

I can almost guarantee you that if today we wanted to find information about 'How to Get Unstuck', we would have several books pop out of a search engine. A stuck visionary must constantly keep reading to gain resilience muscle to shorten the days that he is stuck.

Here is the thing though: You do not just read any book for the sake of it. You have to find resourceful books such like Biographies, Success Principles and such like. You get a book that talks about stories of conquests by people who were in worse situations than yourself. All of a sudden, your pity party will be ruined. In its place (after you have shed a tear or two by inspiration), you will find that you have been energized enough to do something about your situation.

**4. Taking Action:**
This trumps all the methods ever discussed. When stuck, and executive can easily become an emotional wreck. Very many emotions circle around a stuck executive like vultures waiting for him to give up before they pounce for a kill. It has been scientifically proven that emotions are not subject to reason, but they are subject to action. Fear is an emotion. It is not subject to reason. You cannot out-reason fear. You cannot out-maneuver fear by having a strong mind. No, you take mastery over damaged emotions resulting from your stuck situation by taking action…and I would dare say, any action, whether inspired or not is enough to break the cycle of the illusion that the emotions create.

---

*"Champions do something they hate to birth something they love"*
~ Dr. Mike Murdock

---

For good measure, inspired actions would basically come from information gained from questions, mentors and coaches as well as reading books. That is why it is important not to read another book until you have implemented a good percentage of the 'action points' spelt out in the current book. That should tell us that a good book should be informative as well as call us to action. It should be inspiring as well as motivating. An *Inspirational* book might give you goose flesh and cause you to stand in awe of the author. A *motivating* book gives you action points, tools that you can use to change your current situation for the better. Action trumps all.

**5. Focus on Where you are Going:**
One powerful thing that can be done is to keep a vision of your desires before you at all times! At the moment, you are surrounded by doom and gloom, and so you need to be as proactive as possible by gazing at the pictures of where you are going more than eulogizing where you are. I know you are walking on foot to church, yet you have nothing to lose by looking at the photos of your dream car! You have to keep 're-minding' yourself about this again and again. In the process, your mindset get's calibrated in the correct perspective.

Young Ben in his primary school was once axed from being a school official. You know what that meant? It meant going back to do manual labor with the rest of the kids after being a school official for more than a year! That did not stop the young boy from dreaming. He dreamt of being a school official rather than the class prefect he previously was. It did not take a month before one school official messed up... and guess who was selected? Ben! How this young executive forgot this powerful art of visualization beats me. He had never read about it in a book nor had he been instructed about it by an elder. It just came to him like an urge... like a desire. Somehow, Ben had this big self esteem that stemmed from his performance in school and his mum's position as a school teacher in the village. He knew that he deserved better than being a 'common student'. So he visualized. He thought of where he would want to be rather than mourn the fact that his classmates had rejected him as a class prefect.

Focusing on where you are going is a more powerful thing than focusing on the hardship of the present, at least in terms of empowering your mind. If you want to stay obscure, you need not dream of a better tomorrow. You need not remind yourself of the fleeting hardship of today. However, if you want the days of your stuck situation accelerated, you get all the photos of the best outcome, or of where you want to be. Surround yourself with these images. Let them be before you all the time.

Later on, our stuck executive got a baby gal on father's day 2013. During her pregnancy, Ben's wife used this method so powerfully. Ben had no income still. The couple had no idea how they would pay for hospital charges during the delivery of their second born. Ye that did not deter Ben's wife from dreaming about a nice private hospital from which she could deliver. She got photos of a nice private hospital and pasted them on their vision board. It was only after their daughter had been born that she reminded Ben of that fact, after it had come to pass.

It so happened that Ben got another shot to be an executive, and that means that he was able to pay for their hospital charges without a problem... and guess what? It was a private hospital just as his wife had 'ordered'.

You have absolutely nothing to lose when you visualize where you are going. However, images of hardship and brokenness can sap your strength so much and make your stuck situation heavier. Learn to look at where you are going more than focus on where you are!

Before we can take a look at the general attitudes that would help one out of a stuck environment, let us catch up with our stuck executive, Ben, and find out how his life is shaping up.

Ben and his team leader were driven back to the capital city for thorough check-up and treatment. They were treated for bruises and small lacerations on their feet and face. There was no internal bleeding... any broken bones. Two lives spared. Two chances offered again to make a mark in society. Ben's car was towed to the local Police Station and soon enough arrangements were made for its repair.

Life seemed to move on slowly from then on. Ben relied on Public Transportation for a while as his car was being repaired. This, though awkward, was nothing new to Ben. He had used Public Transport pretty much half of his professional life up to now. There was this day that his boss had to travel outside the country... and that offered Ben an opportunity to use his car.

Ben found himself more cautious in driving than he previously had been. They normally say that once beaten, twice shy! Well that was true for Ben. He was even much more careful since the car he was using was not his. Meanwhile, as far as his essence in life was concerned, Ben had nothing documented at this point in time. Life seemed to just pick up from where it was left.

One day, Ben was to make a short trip in the field about 60 Kilometers from the Capital to meet a team member and deliver some crucial documents. He went all by himself on this trip. Midway through the journey, Ben spotted something that on any day would be normal, but not on this one. About 200 meters ahead, several women were crossing the road...and seemed to be followed not so closely by a young girl probably two years old. The girl was stark naked.

There was no problem about that scene, since they had already crossed 75% of the road. Ben was not speeding, so there was nothing to worry about. Then, it happened! It seemed as if the kid and the women were not the same party. It seemed to Ben like one of the women was the girl's mum who did not know that her two-year old girl was faithfully tailing them.

Still it was all good a situation. However, what happened is that as the mum took a simple glance behind her, she noticed something that seemed to absolutely horrify her. Her daughter was on the road following her! Ben was now closing in on the scene…and did not seem to be disturbed by the drama unfolding just ahead of him.

What happened next is beyond anyone's explanation. It seemed to Ben like the child's mum, being horrified that the daughter was following the company, shouted at her child. The child in turn was scared stiff…apparently of being spanked by the mum. Instead of crossing over towards the mum, the child run back right into the middle of the road. By now, Ben was smack right there as the child was crossing back.

To date, Ben does not remember what happened. He says he remembers swerving forcefully to avoid knocking the child. His heart raced. His mind raced. His emotions were blank. His blood cuddled. Ben slowed down and stopped on the road-side, got out of the car and raced back to the kid who was now sprawled on the side of the road.

The mum was screaming, wailing. A crowd was gathering. The child…she was horrified and cried too! That was a good sign. Thank God she was not dead! It turned out that it was the child who actually knocked the side of the car with her heard just as Ben swerved to avoid hitting her! Oh what drama this was!

And you would think that the negligent mum would be repentant of her actions and thank God for sparing her daughter! You would be wrong. What just happened to her was an opportunity to mint money out of Ben. Of course Ben rushed the kid and the mum to hospital, where nothing major was diagnosed. He had to write a statement at the nearby police station and report back later on.

That is when the shameless mum asked for top Dollar. Ben had never been furious at a negligent human being before then. He insisted that he would pay nobody nothing, and if need be, pursue the case in the courts of law.

Ben's state of emotions was not good for negotiations, so a witty colleague had him out of the room and in his absence, they bought the kid's parents some lunch having made them understand that they would lose the case and be charged for negligence.

Another drama in Ben's life goes…and life goes on.

In all indications, there was absolutely nothing else going on in Ben's life save dispensing his duties as an executive. All his life up until that moment was revolving around fulfilling all the requirements stipulated in his Job Description.

This is dangerous living to say the least. Just like a child running in front of a car from out of the blue, so that Job can become redundant for any and many reasons. Ben has come to learn later on that there is nothing called Job security. Job security is an illusion. It's an oxymoron.

It is a handcuff that causes people never to explore their full potential and calling in the world. Days swiftly passed into weeks and weeks into months. Christmas was finally here and Ben found himself driving home for the very first time since he was born. He had left the village on foot, he went back to his village driving…a corporate car! Would you not call that success? Well, I think so. I also do not think so. How many people achieve such a feat? Not so many. That is why you might want to call it success. However, true success would have been if Ben went back driving his own vehicle.

Ben earned lots of respect from the villagers. His parents were more than proud of him. He was useful at the extended family level, especially as they had some small functions going on. Indeed life was good, and Ben thanked God for his fortunes.

The holidays were coming fast to a close…and Ben the expatriate had to make his way back to work. Before he knew it, January was already knocking. Time for strategic planning. Time to review and set new targets. Unbeknown to Ben, this was also the time for life to offer him another cusp…a major one at that.

His organization was on a one year renewable contract. There was absolutely no doubt to anybody that Ben and company had done proud to the product he was championing. Besides, his organization was the only one in the entire world that had experience in handling the product that Ben was championing. There was therefore all indication that work will resume as usual, and Ben would pick up from where he left in the previous year.

That is exactly what Ben did until a week down the line that he received a disturbing Email from his client. He was to hold out all activities until deliberations for the renewal of his company's contract are finalized. That was indeed not so welcoming a message. When Ben passed the information over to his boss and finally to his C.E.O, there was an aura of uneasiness around the organization.

Days of waiting over what seemingly would be something to rubber stamp and move on turned into weeks, and weeks into a month. Meanwhile, Ben's C.E.O was being courted by other organizations in the country for the same business arrangement. Options were being weighed here. Lives were in the balance to say the least.

People always talk about 'the gap'. The gap is the space between two lucrative contracts. What do you do while in the gap? How do you navigate in the gap? That was the million dollar question that Ben's C.E.O had to answer. Meanwhile, Ben, his boss and the rest of the team had to wait with bated breath as the gap grew. Imagine a life on hold?

Honestly…imagine not just Ben's but several lives, about 50 of them on a halt…waiting for someone else to make a decision! What a funny state. While waiting, momentum decreases. While waiting, uncertainty sets in. While waiting, favor diminishes. While waiting, poor decisions can be made…and that is exactly what Ben's C.E.O did.

She made a poor decision, nevertheless a decision in itself. While in the gap, it is imperative that we gather as much information as possible about our next move before we take it. Granted, we need to reduce the period of the gap. The dilemma here is making a decision to be back in action against making a decision to wait for the right action to take.

Once again, questions are great tools to use when you get to the fork on the road. There are some mentors who would tell you that you need to make a decision fast, since you can always adjust it. Well, that normally is true if you are in charge of your own life…and not when your life is partly being controlled by someone else.

Granted, I agree that we need to make decisions as fast as we can. We just need to make sure that all the obvious angles in the decision making equation have been looked into.

Ben's C.E.O did the unimaginable. She wrote to her client organization and terminated her services. People do not fire clients do they? It is normally the other way round. Clients fire providers…for one reason or another. Her next move was to move her services to a competing client…who if she would have just asked around even for an hour, she would have known their history.

They had less pedigree than the client she just fired. They had a history of nonpayment of services. They had court cases with nearly all their service providers either about delays in executing payments or not paying at all. They did not have structure. They lacked passion for their other products.

If we can just back up a little bit, we are not talking about Ben's C.E.O, but about Ben himself. Ben was never a graduate of a University because of this and that. So when this gap came about, Ben was terribly scared about his future. In his own assessment, he lacked options. This book is about nothing else but options. Ben had found safety in his position as an expatriate executive through a promotion. Now that position was threatened because his contract was hanging in the balance.

Unlike his boss who was confident because of his Degree, Ben felt inferior. Ben did not want to look at any options. He resorted to praying that the contract would be renewed. He did not want to leave his boss and venture out to look for something else. Ben was downright scared!

Most scared people never take action. They stay cocooned in their comfort zones. They stay immobilized in fear, and incapacitated to take action in any way. What we need to understand, and what Ben needed to understand is that emotions are never subject to reason…and not even prayer. Emotions are only subject to activity. Taking massive action is what Ben needed to do…yet he felt in that same old trap that is more demonic than anything imagined…he decided to wait!

Waiting effectively emasculates an individual and transfers control of their life to someone else…or to an event or an expectation. Indeed, there are those moments that a soul can only wait, but even then, there are still questions of essence that a soul can seek while waiting.

You should have seen Ben's relief when his C.E.O finally announces the securing of another one year contract. Ben was to continue working in his capacity. Yet it would never be the same. He was ecstatic but just like his C.E.O, he failed to ask questions about where he was heading and what awaited him there.

Ben's beloved team was not amused. Indeed they still wanted to work with Ben…but not with this new organization! They vacillated and dragged their feet. The former organization meanwhile had no choice but to court them back. Here was a team that was in dilemma. It was a time to ask 'what matters now' kind of questions. You bet!

Yet in a period of few days, Ben saw a shifting of allegiances like he had never before. In life people will stick with you as long as it is convenient enough. On the other hand, Ben was kind of happy that at least he had a 'bird in the hand' with the current position. He would keep working as an executive, and by extension, he would still earn. That counted to a very great degree.

Unable to get his once passionate team on board with the next program, Ben conferred with his CEO and then fired all the team members at once. Perfect decision! He took a full week interviewing for the now vacant positions. This was another first for Ben for which the C.E.O really praised him for. It was a bold step.

Work begun in earnest, but there was something missing. The new client was not on board with their own product like the previous client that the C.E.O had dismissed. In all respects, Ben was more passionate about the product he was championing than most of the personnel from his client. It was simply frustrating.

A week turned into a month before a month was half a year. The relationship between Ben's Company and their client was never better. Payments were not being done. Ben was reduced to the role of a debt collector. This made him sick to the stomach.

Finally, the client cancelled the contract they had with Ben's Company. One sullen evening, Ben's C.E.O called and started reassuring Ben that all was well, but that the Company should cease its operations with immediate effect.

Ben felt that tight knot in his stomach. His heart beat so fast, he started sweating. Fear gripped him so hard. The very fear that he had been running away from all this time by clinging on the said position. In fact Ben was so afraid that he kept clinging on his position. At the deepest core of his heart, this executive knew that it would never ever be the same again. His fears were with him in a real fury.

What do you do when life hits you with a curve ball? What do you do when you get to the crossroads of your life? What do you do when your step is slippery and you find yourself forced to fall to the bottom of the pit?

Well, Ben did not have any answers, just like most people would.

The major problem is that we mostly consider the answers to be outside of ourselves. So we start looking outside. We start looking for another opportunity to stay relevant in life. If per chance we consider ourselves a little inferior in qualifications, we retreat into a self condemning shell. We never look for opportunities any more. We start looking for miracles.

We think that a miracle, which in this case we define to be something that will go against our odds and give us a break in our stuck situation, we think that it is all we need. That is exactly what Ben did.

As much as he did not lose his job that day, he was the only employee left to help keep the company afloat. This had happened to Ben before. When he did have that pathetic attitude at his first full time job after years of being stuck in it, he was passed on a promotion to a new complex that the company had taken. Ben was left behind ostensibly to oversee the closure of the company over a period of months. History repeats itself!

In other words, Ben's job then was to oversee his joblessness in few months. Talk of dying in installments! The same thing that Ben faced then is exactly what he is facing now. Ben was lost for options since he regarded himself inferior having no University Degree. He did not seek any chance outside of what he had. He never figured that he would prosper if he did. So he started asking for miracles.

It turned out that the same company wing that he was set to oversee closure started prospering much more than the new one. Never mind that they had taken the very best resources to the new complex. Never mind that they did not give Ben a hoot on what he needed even for a day.

But this was not to be in Ben's new assignment. There was no turn around. Ben did absolutely nothing to get new business for his company…because he was scared!

Before long, Ben who was now getting married got information from the Company's accountant that he would be receiving half of his Salary from that moment on. The decline of this heralded expatriate was now on! Still, Ben prayed and waited for a miracle. None came. He increased his prayer time, his fasting. No change happened.

Ben's single source of income—a salary was drying up and fast. Getting that half salary was becoming a difficult thing. But that is obvious. The company was receiving nothing from Ben's efforts while at the same time babysitting him. The C.E.O was right in halving his salary. It was needed pressure. Pressure is good to get us from our comfort zones and do something.

Contrary to our feelings pressure is not an indication that all is closing in on us. Pressure is a blessing that tells us that the world would like the best out of us! Ben had never been taught to embrace pressure. All his life, it is like he had been on a quest for a foolproof way of avoiding pressure at all costs. This is an exercise in futility!

In fact it is when we apply pressure on ourselves that we really start getting ahead of the pack. When we force ourselves to do that which is unpopular with our flesh, when we force ourselves persistently right out of our comfort zones, we grow exponentially. Pressure comes in two ways: First, it comes our way mostly as the final beckon from life for us to do something about our meaning. Second, a visionary smells the highs and downs from afar and continually reviews their lives, forcing the pressure on themselves.

Clearly, Ben waited for the pressure to come. The paradox with this kind of waiting is that normally, people wait for the problem not to come. In the end it does come, and when it arrives, someone is already too late to launch a comeback. This waiting in a way digs up a big hole that is increasingly hard to get out of. It is the formation of being stuck proper…this waiting.

On the other hand, visionaries do not wait for the beckoning pressure to come…they go meet it head on! Their minds are settled that life is not a straight line. It is an up and down curve. Life consists of troughs and tops right from birth. Therefore, you can as well accept it and learn to master the challenges thrown your way at the earliest opportunity.

Ben did not know of a very potent tool that he could use at that moment in time. It is the use of what I call W.C.S. (Worst Case Scenario). Operating from the earliest opportunity at the level of the worst case scenario is what Ben needed…not just in this situation, but also in the previous situation at his first job. Clearly he has not learnt. Either that or he is simply scared!

> *"If we just acknowledged the bad situation sooner, it would often be less painful to resolve. It would be cheaper, the circumstances might be more beneficial, the problems would be easier to solve, we could be more honest with everyone concerned, we would feel better about ourselves, and we would certainly have more integrity. But we have to get past our denial"*
> –Jack Canfield, The Success Principles

True, operating from the worst case scenario is not a bed of roses. It is not a comfortable place. It is a place of very many unknowns. Here is the thing.

One way or another, the worst case scenario will be here, as long as you have smelt it. You either accept it at the earliest opportunity and move head on to tackle it, or you wait for it to come find you unprepared.

You will do yourself a great favor if you stopped to take a stock of things the way they are right now. You will do great for your own sake to assume the W. C. S of your situation or situations and start working from that position. The goal setting Guru Brian Tracy says, "The Best way to Predict the Future is to create it". And you create it right here and now by accepting the 'forthcoming harsh reality' and adjusting your sails from where you are. Remember the Titanic? They called it 'Unsinkable'. Some even went to say that even God could not sink it. Fact: The Titanic was unsinkable based on the technology that was used to make it…provided it avoided icebergs. They received several warnings about icebergs ahead their voyage…but they chose to ignore, opting to put their faith, hope and trust in the psychological fact that the ship was unsinkable.

I will ask again. What warning signs have you received of late? What are you doing about them? Praying? Hoping? Rebuking them?

## CHAPTER FOUR:
# The Dark Side of Hope

*"Hope is essential, without it, life is a daunting task"*
—Kim George

At what time in our lives should we hope? This is an important question to ask. Hope alone can carry people through very tough situations. Hope is a virtue. Yet there is the dark side of it. If you met someone who has given up hope, it might be that hope never served them in the first place.

Here is the thing though; you cannot blame hope on their giving up. You can only blame them! I will explain that later. Let us now re-visit Ben's story as it develops into a typical stuck state.

So far, Ben who is scared to death because of his perceived inadequacies is on a half salary. He is being paid technically to close down the company's operations in the foreign country. The countdown has begun. No, it actually did begin the very time there was an issue with the first contract.

*"Our deepest fear is not that we are inadequate.*
*Our deepest fear is that we are powerful beyond measure.*
*It is our light not our darkness that most frightens us.*
*We ask ourselves, who am I to be brilliant, gorgeous,*
*talented and fabulous?*

*Actually, who are you not to be?*
*You are a child of God.*
*Your playing small does not serve the world.*
*There's nothing enlightened about shrinking so that other*
*people won't feel insecure around you.*

*We were born to make manifest the glory of*
*God that is within us.*

*It's not just in some of us; it's in everyone.*
*And as we let our own light shine,*
*we unconsciously give other people*
*permission to do the same.*

*As we are liberated from our own fear,*
*Our presence automatically liberates others".*

—Marianne Williamson

So what strategy was Ben using to either avoid being stuck or to get out of the 'maze' he was in at the moment? You guessed it! Ben used the strategy of hope. He relegated his triumph over his predicament to time. He started po-

> "The spiritual never took over the empirical without the participation of humans... There has got to be some balance between our spiritual activity and the using of our heads to think and do what we can do at the moment in time".

sitioning himself for a miracle. He prayed more. He fasted more. He was faithful in his giving. He was more sensitive to God unlike the previous months when he was a real executive.

Granted, all these now heightened spiritual practices should be part and parcel of Ben's everyday life. I would bet that most people when they find themselves in a crisis, they do resort to spiritual solace over their physical or material challenges. This is exactly what Ben is employing at his critical phase in life. Is it wrong to do this?

Now that is another interesting question. Spiritually mature people will tell you that most of life is dictated in spiritual realms. However, the spiritual never took over the empirical without the participation of humans. This is what I mean. There has got to be some balance between our spiritual activity and the using of our heads to think and do what we can do at the moment in time.

When Ben resorts to an all out spiritual assault to his practical problem, he is just doing one part of the equation, hoping that the other part will take care of itself. Nothing can be further from the truth! I heard a preacher some years back say that "Balance is the ability to go to both extremes equally!" I couldn't agree more. Ben's focus to solve his stuck situation was not balanced. It was good yes, but it was not balanced!

So we need to ask ourselves this question. Is it wrong to hope? Remember we are yet to answer the opening question of this chapter: At what time should we hope? Was Ben wrong in applying this strategy? You see, your answer to this question will reveal your resilience index. If you would say that this was the correct strategy for Ben to apply, chances are that you are just as scared as Ben was in his stuck condition.

> "Life without fear doesn't last very long--you'll be run over by a bus (or a boss) before you know it. The fearless person, on the other hand, sees the world as it is (fear included) and then makes smart (and brave) decisions".
> ——Seth Godin

For the record, hoping is a good thing. We should hope at all times! In fact, we should never ever lose hope. Yet hope alone is not a strategy! Let me repeat: Hope is not a strategy! Here is whom hope is for:

- Hope is for the prepared,
- Hope is for those who have done something towards it's attainment
- Hope is for those who are exploring each and every option
- Hope is for those who have developed character of resilience.
- Hope is for those in motion
- Hope if for those whose next step is beyond any power they have on earth (and there are many)
- Hope is not for those who do nothing.
- Hope is not for the wishful thinkers.
- Hope is not for those who lack a primary strategy.
- Hope is not a strategy!

I think Ben' story will put all this in perspective. When the contract was lost, he resorted to hope. Nothing better happened. Then his salary was halved. What did he do? He hoped even the more. He started working more on his spiritual faith than on anything. Meanwhile, life kept giving him all these serious wake-up calls. Ben was now married and actually expecting their first born son. His salary was not enough. Of course the company still paid his house rent. That made things a little bit easier…yet that was just momenta rily.

A time came when, naturally, the company could no longer continue running losses. What company pays for an employee month in and out who does not provide value to it? Let's just face it. The sole purpose of Business organizations like the one Ben worked for is to make profits…and of course minimize expenses. The expenses on Ben were totally unwarranted. Nothing came from his end.

---

*"Hope works when it keeps people engaged"*
–Kim George

---

The C.E.O gave Ben an ultimatum. In exactly three month's time, the company would fold its operations and retreats from the foreign market .We all know what that meant to Ben. It meant no income. It meant no more company car. It meant no more rent being paid by someone else. It meant that unless Ben's strategy of hope worked, Ben would effectively be poor.

- Debts would beckon.
- Stress would beckon.
- Disillusionment would beckon

- Productivity would be nonexistent.
- Forget about leaving a legacy on earth, you have got a wife and a child to feed!
- Life would become mundane.
- Did that happen?

Yes it did, and it happened to a major degree that literally ate away Ben's *essence* like some wasting disease. Shortly, what used to be a mere backdrop that did not abuse the senses became such a serious struggle to Ben. He became late in paying his bills. In fact, several times his electricity supply was cut off. In the previous months, the electricity bill was paid with loose change. Today, that loose change is so purely precious for baby's food.

The big one came. Ben could not pay his rent. The first month went. Of course again, he never explained to the landlord what was going on. The landlord knew Ben had a stable job. He knew there some disturbances here and there. Ben had been very faithful paying the rent. So naturally, the landlord gave him the benefit of doubt.

Two months unpaid rent piled up to three…then four! While previously Ben would buy necessities from the supermarket nearby, right now he was one of the biggest borrowers. Of course it was easy for someone who paid cash for commodities to have credit facilities extended to him. He had a pedigree. However, this also started fading…the credibility that is.

---

*"Every time we choose safety, we reinforce f e a r"*
~Cheri Huber

---

Meanwhile, what was Ben doing to rectify the situation? Well, like many other people the world over, especially Christians, Ben prayed, hoped, fasted and waited for a miracle. He should have learnt that by now! Miracles do not just happen, do they? No they don't!

Let's talk about that for a minute. Now, this is as controversial as it gets. Over the past few months, I have been asking my coaching clients one question, and I will ask it here again. "When is the last time you experienced a miracle in your life?" I do not know about you, but for the most part, if at all they did experience a miracle, it is in the distant past. Now, I know that this can be a thoroughly controversial topic…however; I will say what I have to say about miracles.

First off, God is more of a goal-setter than a miracle worker. To my knowledge, a miracle is a supernatural intervention in exceptional natural circumstances that literally freezes or shortens time and removes all the side effects. Picture this: if God wanted the whole earth to be filled up when he said "be fruitful and multiply"...don't you think he would have had the power to make that immediate? Don't you think he would have made us all at once?

> *"Waiting is an acknowledgement of divine timing"*
> —Dr. Mike Murdock

The fact is, He had the power. He had the authority...and the last time I checked, He still does. However, in his infinite wisdom He chose to do it the way He did. Let me ask you another question. Given the opportunity (and looking back in retrospect), would you rather that mankind developed in phases all through the ages, or that we all appeared on the planet at the same time, waving iPads, and experiencing the greatest advancement in technology today? Your answer to this question will most definitely locate you.

Nature has a way of teaching us stuff. We know through science that for a beautiful butterfly to come out of the pupa stage, it has to struggle. If you 'help' it out, you basically are killing the process and the butterfly with it. God is such a mighty miracle worker that he set all systems in place and never has He ever gone back to fix the systems! This speaks of seeds and seasons. It talks of process.

Yes, He did create everything at once, but has allowed seasons and systems to churn out the results. And so should it be in our lives. The biggest balancing act that our lives are made of involves knowing these systems, putting them into use against praying to God for a miraculous intervention. Most people would rather that a miracle happens in their life... and that includes me. However, I have come to learn that there are no miracles that happen arbitrarily. I have also come to realize that miracles are and can be a daily occurrence...if we intend them to be.

> *"The biggest balancing act that our lives are made of involves knowing these systems, putting them into use against praying to God for a miraculous intervention... No miracle was ever performed primarily so that man can be comfortable. A miracle simply puts man back in his best fit to fulfill the original purposes of God on his life".*

No miracle was ever performed primarily so that man can be comfortable. A miracle simply puts man back in his best fit to fulfill the original purposes of God on his life. I read somewhere that 'miracles become commonplace few days after they have occurred'. That tells you that process and systems are of higher value than miracles.

> *"A curse is always on the unused talent"*
> —Dr. Mike Murdock

Do you know the other name used for miracles? Luck! As I write this book while based in Uganda, very many Banks and Mobile Network Operators are seriously cashing on this 'hope' that people have. In fact, one giant Mobile Network Operator in Kenya, Safaricom has mastered leveraging on hope. That is why each year, they run a 'competition' of sorts where over 20 people are made 'millionaires' in a space of three months.

Let me ask this: Who would not want to do a simple transaction in a Bank or with a Telecom company and win some dollars? Nearly everyone hopes for this to happen. A great percentage of people believe in luck! But look at the odds! In Kenya for example, there are over 15 Million (conservative estimate by the time of writing) Safaricom subscribers. The strategy of hope says that you are betting your life with a chance of over one in a million to become a millionaire in three months!

This is all wrong. Now, let me say this: If I happened to be in that country and randomly I am the lucky winner, do you think I will walk around rejecting the 'strategy of hope'? Hardly! I will be a happy family man I assure you. But that is just the thing…it is a random chance!

So you have the masses in the strategy of hope doing repeated transactions to attract some luck. Of course the winners normally call it a miracle! Heck there are people whose prayer items includes winning the lottery! However, as we have seen…even if God was in the picture, Safaricom is just awarding 20 out of 15 Million. Do you really think God will be involved in making the 15 Million Millionaires through Safaricom? Think again!

So let us put this in perspective. Hope, according to Wikipedia, is the state which promotes belief in a good outcome related to events and circumstances in one's life. Hope is a state, not a strategy! The word state means stationary as you might have guessed it.

> *"The producers of hope do what they can do with or without hope...*
> *producers create their own luck, consumers wait for luck to happen"*
> –Kim George

So when Ben resorts to thinking that all the 'he has left' is to believe and hope, he couldn't be more wrong! Let me say that hope will serve in the interim. In fact, one of the most powerful things you can have in your life is a heightened state of hope.

- A hopeful soul is creative
- A hopeful soul is happy
- A hopeful soul is energetic
- A hopeful soul is good company

My point is that the *state of hope* is a very big *catalyst* for success. Hope alone is not a complete strategy, hope is a catalyst. The mistake that Ben is doing at the moment is relegating all of his massive life to a state and a catalyst of success whereas he is not doing anything to actualize his desires! This state kept Ben *'safe'*. He knew that some time later, a miracle would happen. So he *waited* for it. As long as he could just put food on the table *while waiting*, that would do. And that is what it did.

Ben's wife however would not be initially drawn into this strategy. She asked Ben some questions about their finances. Ben sweated bullets but could not give an answer other than 'things will be better'. Well the question is: How are things going to be better if we do nothing about them? For some reason, Ben was able to convince his wife that God would come through for them.

> *"If we continue to pursue hope, then we had best become a producer of it,*
> *rather than a consumer of it".*
> –Peter Block

Yet I believe that God sent Ben's wife as another 'messenger' to stir him up in his thinking. Her queries were another hint to Ben that he was resorting into the life of 'comfort'. He did not want to face things head on. His head was in the clouds, blind to the truth. The goggles of faith he wore totally obliterated the hopeless reality around him.

Who is in control? Who should be in Control?

Women as we know it are made of a different crop. Women's greatest need is safety. She wants to know how her child will eat. She wants to know how her child will wear and she wants to know how the child will go to school. A great woman will be greatly unsettled if there is no assurance of safety and provision. Ben's wife knew how incredible her husband was: gifted, smart, astute, wise. Yet she did not know one thing: Ben was scared because of his inadequacies!

Despite the assurance that Ben was giving his wife, he faced one stiff controversy between his mental assent of hope and the deep down dissonance in his heart that all was not well. Somehow, Ben knew that hope was not a strategy, but he still believed it was.

Let us analyze for a minute how the illusion of hope works.

Look at the following statement:

*"I really hope that things will change for the better".*

Let me ask this question: I know you have not met whoever said the above, but would you please give a description of this person from that statement?

Take a minute or so and think about it. How would you describe the owner of that statement? I am sure that you will not know their name, their marital status, their location in the world, whether they are black or white, whether they have a job or not. As you go on thinking about their description, I am sure you will not know details about their assets, their finances, or their friends.

This however is a given. In your description, you will see someone who exhibits the following characteristics:

- Helplessness,
- Wishful
- Not in control or in charge of their outcome
- Without options
- Relying on something/someone 'outside' for help.

Ladies and gentlemen, above is the plain presentation of the dark side of hope. The dark side of hope robs everyone who uses hope as a strategy of the ability to do what they can do at the moment. It transfers the power to do to someone else, be it God, a friend or a relative.

This effectively means that you are not any way in control of your outcome. *Think about that paradox. You need an outcome, you are not in control of that outcome yet that is the strategy you are employing—powerlessness!*

> *"In its worst form, hope is a negation of our greatness and what we do have"*
> —Kim George

My mentor Dr. Mike Murdock normally finds great fault in this Christian cliché, "God is in control!" In fact, that statement alone has created more Atheists than it has comforted believers. The idea that God is in control would really negate very many things.

- If God was in control, why does He need prayer?
- If God was in control, why does tragedy to befall mankind?
- If God was in control, why doesn't he protect our women and children from rapists?
- If God was in control, why does He need me?
- If God was in control, why did He create humans?
- If God was in control, what is He really controlling?

The statement that "God is in control" creates more powerlessness than it creates solutions to the challenges we are facing right now. It tells us that the best we can do at the moment is of no value to what God can do. Now that is technically true, since no man can compete with God's power.

> *"God will never give you something to do where he is unnecessary in the equation"*
> ——Dr. Mike Murdock

## What Can You Do?

*However, the God I know works through man.* In other words, while man is waiting on God, for the most part, God is waiting on man! What is it that you can do? It is what you can do that God uses to amplify the results. Look through the scriptures and see.

- God used Abraham's faith and availability
- God used the rod that Moses had in his hand
- God used Joseph's dreams
- God used David's skill and attitude
- God used Peter's availability
- God used Paul's theological knowledge to make him an Apostle to the Gentiles

- God used what was available from man in the miracles of feeding the multitudes

Even when God says He has an open door, it would still be utterly useless if the one for whom the door is opened does not go through it!

**Newsflash:** Relying on hope with the Illusion that God is in control is the sure way or robbing yourself on doing what you can do!

> *"David did not kill Goliath on his knees and Nehemiah did not build the wall on his knees; he prayed to his God and then went out to build it"*
> –Peter J. Daniels

It is just that small thing. What you can do. God is not asking you to move mountains! Even when He does, He tells you to use faith (remember faith without action is dead) as small as a mustard seed. Small things. Small actions. What is it that you can do?

It is the concept of what we can do that has revolutionized our times.

Blind people would not read if we employed the strategy of hope…waiting for a miracle. But with the concept of what we can do, we have come up with Braille.

Deaf and dumb people would not be able to communicate, read and write. But with what we can do, there are hundreds of thousands of schools for these special people.

The paralytics cannot participate in the Olympics, but with a big heart of Dr. Ludwig Guttman, the Paralympics Summer games are the second largest sporting event in the entire world.

Not every child is an A student academically, but with the concept of what we can do, we have seen geniuses in other fields like music, art and extra-curricular activities.

In fact, not everyone has a degree but with what they can do, we have seen better managers with no degrees than those with degrees.

*In essence, what we are saying is that the bulk of life, more than 90% of it finds meaning and essence in what we can do in the wake of seeming impossibilities.* What keeps mankind going is what man can do at the moment. That is why we did not have Internet at creation, sliced bread in 1920, Cell Phones in 1950, and android phones in 1979 but life did sizzle those days!

## Laws and Virtues

It would therefore be of great disservice to any soul, whether stuck or otherwise to think of hope alone as a strategy for getting to the next level. We as the human race have never achieved any advancement worth noting on the strategy of hope. It has never worked, it never will work and when you come to the crux of the matter, it was never intended to work!

> *"Life is under no obligation to give us what we expect"*
> —Margaret Mitchell

> *"In essence, what we are saying is that the bulk of life, more than 90% of it finds meaning and essence in what we can do in the wake of seeming impossibilities. What keeps mankind going is what man can do at the moment. That is why we did not have Internet at creation, sliced bread in 1920, Cell Phones in 1950, and android phones in 1979 but life did sizzle those days"!*

I have never in my entire life heard about the 'Law of Hope'. Have you? Yet I have heard about the Law of Gravity, the Laws of Success, the Principles of Success, the Law of Critical Mass and so on. There is a heaven and earth difference between Laws and virtues. We honestly need both. Without laws, there is chaos and disorder. Without laws, there is no progress. That is why it is thoroughly stupid and foolish for a human being so structured even in their body system alone to believe that the world came out of a big bang!

I nearly wrote big bhang, because I think smoking lots of bhang makes you come up with such like theories. The world is held together by Laws and Principles. In the Book of Genesis the Eighth Chapter and Verse 22, God tells Noah the following:

> *"For as long as Earth lasts, planting and harvest, cold and heat, summer and winter, day and night will never stop."*

God, in essence was telling humanity that to the degree that you use the laws of nature to your advantage, to that degree will you succeed or fail! Most people including Ben are using just one side of God, the side of virtues: Hope, Love, Goodness, Humility and so on thinking that that is all that is needed to succeed. Ben has done this several times. In fact I dare say that the some of the most super-spiritual people are so prone to fall in this trap. By the way, when you actually get to it, you will realize that these virtues are mostly exercised through action, such actions that are subject to Laws and Principles.

How come some 'Missionaries' are one of the poorest people? They are honest. They are filled with God's virtues. They are even smack in the middle of the work of God! How come they are struggling with their finances? Chances are that they are using one side of God!

This reminds me of Ben's Dad. We already saw that Ben's dad became a minister of the gospel of Jesus Christ later on in his life. Did that change their family's economic condition? Hardly! A typical use of one side of God came right through when Ben was in College. Colleges need students to pay tuition. It so happened that Ben had not paid his tuition and the College would not let him in unless of course the arrears were settled.

> *"Think about it. No parent ever wakes up in the morning and says to his or her mate, "I've just figured out three more ways we can mess up our kid." Parents are always doing the best they can to be good parents. But the combination of their own psychological wounds, their lack of knowledge and parenting skills, and the pressures of their lives often converge and create behaviors that hurt us. It was not personal to you. They would have done the same thing to anyone who was in your shoes at that moment. The same is true for everyone else ...all the time"*
> –Jack Canfield, The Success Principles

So this is what happened. Ben's dad dressed in his priestly regalia and took Ben to see the School Master. Ben was so embarrassed that day. His dad's bargaining chip was that he was a priest and he said it as much, just in case the School Officials missed his Collar. So here is a servant of God relying not on God's Laws of success and prosperity but relying completely on the virtues. That is where Ben inherently received his mentoring from.

There was that particular time in Ben's life where he was so fed up with his first job that he wanted to quit. That feeling happened to coincide with a bizarre decision in the organization that he worked for to obliterate a retainer salary and put everyone on a commission. Why was it bizarre? Well because Ben was never a salesperson. His job was tutoring at the office. His working hours were from seven in the morning to Eight at night. Pray tell me, how would he get time to go make sales for him to earn a commission?

> *"Often hope alone, can't do for you what you can do for yourself*
> ——Kim George

When this decision was made, Ben's earnings plummeted like a wrongly built house falling to rubble. Would you believe it that a man's monthly salary would be less than USD 50? Am talking about a *monthly* pay! When something like that happens, once again it is a major hint that you need to move! What did Ben do? You guessed it. He invested all of his energies on virtues! At that moment, he stayed with his dad who was a minister in the local church.

**Hope *alone* is not a Complete Strategy**
At one point, the dad wanted to connect Ben to some of his cronies for a job. He kept asking Ben for his CV but Ben, his head high up in the spiritual clouds thought it not useful enough. He considered His God bigger than his dad's friends. He actually wanted to get a job through a miracle: no help from a human being! This is the classic example of the dark side of hope! Did that job come? Of course not!

Hope, ladies and gentlemen, is not a Principle. Hope is not a law! You can therefore never put all your expectations on success and navigating out of a stuck position using a virtue of hope *alone*! It does not work! Well, take a look at your life too. How has hope been of help to you? Are there moments that you totally banked on hope *alone* and it worked? Once again, the miracle that you received, was it totally dependent on hope or on something non-spiritual that you did? Those are good questions to ask oneself.

> *"At one point, the dad wanted to connect Ben to some of his cronies for a job. He kept asking Ben for his CV but Ben, his head high up in the spiritual clouds thought it not useful enough. He considered His God bigger than his dad's friends. He actually wanted to get a job through a miracle: no help from a human being"!*

> "Success is not a miracle, it's a decision"
> –Dr. Mike Murdock

Now, I have to be careful here. Just so incase am labeled a heretic or unbeliever, let me say that virtues are needed. They are good. Yet it is the Bible that says this most famous statement:

> *"Isn't it obvious that God-talk without God-acts is outrageous nonsense?"*
> —James 2:7 (MSG)

In other words, it is Ok to have hoped…but that is not all that is required of a human being. Peter Block said it well that if we are going to use hope, we better be producers of hope and not consumers of it. You cannot produce hope while waiting!

> *"Indecision piles up the odds against you. The more you delay in making a move, the greater the force you will need to employ in getting out of a crisis. The opposite is also true. The earlier a path is taken, a path that is not fully dependent on the waiting strategy of hope, the easier it is to navigate from a stuck situation".*

Ben had this skewed form of thinking that if he took an action, it would mean that he is not a man of faith. His thinking told him that he would be trying to help God! So he stayed in a frozen state of waiting for miracles. Meanwhile, the situation at hand continued to deteriorate.

Ben's self esteem went South. His wife's short lived marital bliss started to wane. Ben was still holed up in his house, waiting and praying. One thing about adversity is that it can easily eat up one's self confidence, especially if the strategy being applied for cure is the strategy of hope.

If we will have a strong resilience index, we need to be 'masters of adversity' if you will. This means that we need to know that man is born to trouble as sure as sparks fly upwards. That means that we need to anticipate adversity.

They say that to be forewarned is to be forearmed. It is this anticipation that helps you to generate options. A strong resilience index is generated by the ability to respond decisively on the entire wake up calls that we get in life. To date, Ben has done absolutely nothing on any of the entire wake up calls in his life, whether great or small. Is it any wonder that he is totally stuck?

**The Results of Indecision**
Employing the strategy of hope as the sole strategy results to one major enemy of success: indecision! *The degree of a crisis in one's life can be directly proportional to the level of indecisiveness in their lives.* For example, it is more than one year since Ben had a wakeup call… when the contract was not renewed. If Ben had acted then, he would have increased his level of resilience index by far.

Indecision piles up the odds against you. The more you delay in making a move, the greater the force you will need to employ in getting out of a crisis. The opposite is also true. The earlier a path is taken, a path that is not fully dependent on the waiting strategy of hope, the easier it is to navigate from a stuck situation.

Eventually, Ben had to close down his organizations operations and drive the company car back. One Wednesday morning, he received a call from the

Company's Human Resource personnel. He was not calling from the head office, he was already in Ben's country. He had already talked to an organization that would organize moving of the office furniture from the country.

Ben was effectively a man with no control of what has happening around him, yet with a big title. Life was giving back to Ben what he had sowed relentlessly—not taking control. We already know that Ben is broke, down and out. When you are not producing anything, nobody wants to be your friend. No one wants to be associated with you. No one calls you…unless of course they are collecting their debts. No one puts you in control of anything.

> *"Most of the shadows in this life are caused by standing in one's own sunshine"*
> –Ralph Waldo Emerson

When all the processes had been finished, Ben returned to his wife with only USD 20 in his pocket! Can you imagine that? A man has been an executive for more than two years, and at the end of that period of time, he only has USD 20 to show for it! Talk of being stuck!

In all honesty, everything seemed so against Ben at that moment. In fact, everything seemed so against Ben that the only plausible method he would use to get out of the setback was the strategy of hope! He felt so powerless. He felt so afraid. He felt so stuck. He had seemingly run out of options. The paradox is that he never generated any options to use apart from the illusion of hope.

The thing about resilience is that it works best when you are actively doing something. You cannot be resilient in waiting (if that is not the only available option). You can only be resilient in working. So as we can see, Ben's strategy of waiting has failed miserably. I am sure that we are not just talking about Ben here. I am sure we are talking about scores of people and organizations across the globe.

## Why People Employ the Strategy of Hope

To be fair, sometimes the strategy of hope does deliver. The only problem (and perhaps the major problem here) is that no one has any direct control on the outcome of the strategy of hope. It is an external thing.

> *"The most important thing in the world is… to distinguish between divine decisions… and your decisions"*
> – Dr. Mike Murdock

So what we need to ask ourselves is this one question. Why do many people employ the strategy of hope?

From Ben's story, I am sure we have already seen that the biggest reason for resorting to hope is the feeling of **inadequacy**. The more people feel inadequate, the more they feel powerless, the more they are prone to depend on something or someone other than themselves to sort out an issue.

The second reason why many people resort to the strategy of hope is pure old **ignorance**. This comes for the most part from what we call super-spirituality. We have seen that Ben also suffered greatly with this one. Ben at one point thought that doing something for himself was proof of lack of faith that God was able to do it for him. He felt like he was 'helping' God, and that is a demonstration of lack of faith! Nothing could be further from the truth.

The third reason as to why people resort to hope is this big one—**fear**. Fear has a way of incapacitating people. It is a big killer. One thing about fear is that it will always be there. There is no one on the face of the earth who never had fear. Courage is not absence of fear. Courage is action in spite of fear. That is what courage is. When people are afraid, fear takes the role of sapping strength from them that they cannot think and they cannot act. Another thing about fear is that what we fear seldom happens. Fear for the most part is an illusion of our worst imaginations.

Do you want to know the remedy for fear? It is the exact opposite of the strategy of hope—taking bold and inspired actions! When you resort to do only what you can in the moment, you begin to neutralize fear. You begin to build a strong resilience. Ben has learnt that in a stuck situation, it is not inspiration that will spur him to action, it is in fact action that will result in inspiration.

Lastly, many people resort to the strategy of hope because **they assume that there are no options to work with!** This I think is the biggest reason for the strategy of hope. When you think that 'there is nothing I can do' then that's just it for you. You will do nothing. The notion that there are no options is an illusion. There is always something you can do.

---

*"Sometimes if you want to change things for the better you have to take things into your own hands."*
—Clint Eastwood

---

We all know the story of Victor Frankl, a man who faced death in the concentration camps organized by Hitler. He knew death every day. His family members were systematically killed. He was a prisoner. He was in chains every single day. Yet, Victor came out saying that he had a choice to make daily about his happiness. He said that nobody could control his moods. At the very least, Victor had an option!

I know very many people reading this book are not in a concentration camp. At the same time, I have no idea what level of crisis you might find yourself in. Some people might have gone without food for days. Some might have been thrown out of their houses (like Ben was later on). Some people might have given up on their career. Some might have settled for less. Some might have lost their marriages, their investments, and their status in society. Some indeed might have lost their sole breadwinner in the family.

> "Things my come to those who wait, but only things left by those who hustle"
> –Abraham Lincoln

I do not know what you are going through, yet this one thing I know: No one should ever tell you that you have no options!! And at the very least, you should never believe the lie that you have no options! It is a lie. You have myriads of options that you can use in the wake of you getting stuck. Now, am not saying that it is easy… neither Am I saying that it is simple…but I am saying that getting out of that stuck situation is massively possible and immensely worth your very life!

*"I know very many people reading this book are not in a concentration camp. At the same time, I have no idea what level of crisis you might find yourself in. Some people might have gone without food for days. Some might have been thrown out of their houses (like Ben was later on). Some people might have given up on their career. Some might have settled for less. Some might have lost their marriages, their investments, and their status in society. Some indeed might have lost their sole breadwinner in the family…*

*I do not know what you are going through, yet this one thing I know: No one should ever tell you that you have no options!! And at the very least, you should never believe the lie that you have no options! It is a lie".*

Even when you have employed the strategy of hope and it has led you to being stuck, you should never believe that you have totally run out of options and that there is nothing that you can do! *The only person who has run out of options is a dead man!*

## CHAPTER 5:

# The Beauty of Adversity

*"Disney, CNN, MTV, Hyatt, Burger King, FedEx, Microsoft, Apple, Gillette, AT&T, Texas Instruments, 20th Century Fox, IBM, Merck, Hershey's, IHOP, Eli Lilly, Coors, Bristol-Myers, Sun, Amgen, The Jim Henson Company, LexisNexis, Autodesk, Adobe, Symantec, Electronic Arts, Fortune, GE, and Hewlett-Packard.*

*These iconic companies were all founded during periods of economic Recession"*

—Report by Sarah Caron

> *"Adversity is like a strong wind. I don't mean just that it holds us back from places we might otherwise go. It also tears away from us all but the things that cannot be torn, so that afterward we see ourselves as we really are, and not merely as we might like to be."*
>
> - Arthur Golden, Memoirs of a Geisha

To say that Ben completely depended on the strategy of hope would not be wholly true. We already know that Ben had come to realize his passion in empowering people. He had started reading motivational books and listening to motivational tapes.

These things really helped him while he was still an executive. Ben got so engrossed in studying the vast potential of the human soul. His pet subject became the purpose of life. He not only so much sought to understand his life's purpose, but he also realized the vast majority of people did not know their purposes. At one point in time, one of Ben's biggest spiritual mentor marveled at Ben's quest for purpose that she confessed that she did not know her 'why'.

Ben had never heard of the title "Life Coach" ever in his life…yet as he continued in his relentless research on the subject of Life Purpose, that word came up repeatedly. He hungered ravenously to be in touch with a Life Coach… and even to become one. That became his unending passion. Ben would cry when he thought about it. He wanted it so bad, that he literally became all ears, tuned up to pick up any vibe in his environment or across the globe about Life Coaching.

By and by, as we have already seen, he started motivating his team members, while he was still an executive. The results were seen of course. Then one day Ben and his fiancé Bernice attended a wedding ceremony at a hotel in the outskirts of the city. Bernice had been invited to sing for the couple.

Ben got hungry and sought for food. In the process, he spotted someone wearing a shirt printed on "Coach" at the back. Of course he was imagination was pricked.

"That is an interesting T-shirt you are wearing. Where can I get one?" Ben asked the stranger. "Oh, this was made by my wife", replied the stranger.

"So I take it that you are a Coach then?" Ben offered.

"Absolutely!" replied the stranger.

And that was the beginning of a very fruitful relationship with Pete, who is now Ben's Coach. Pete is one of the leading corporate Coaches in the country. As Ben continued his relationship with Pete, he also started gathering his own data for coaching. He read extensively… and started writing at the same time.

And then it happened… Coach Pete had Sam one of his protégés launching a monthly event. Pete was invited and naturally he called upon Ben to accompany him. The event was not all that top notch as Ben would have expected. Yet Coach Pete's protégé was doing what he could do. Ben's circle of influence had started growing. It so happened one day that the Coach was invited again by Sam. He was not able to make it and so Ben was recommended to stand in!

> *"Sure, listening to your fears will keep you "safe"…But it will also keep you STUCK"*
> ~ Noah St. John

Ben did such a splendid job that one of the audience members invited him for another function. At that function, there was a Rotary Club President who was so blessed with Ben's talk that she invited him to his club…before long, Ben was becoming the wild card of Rotary Club meeting guest speaker.

He went one step ahead, he started coaching some selected people and charging them for the coaching classes! One person would recommend another. The Coaching Practice for Ben had started increasing tremendously. By the way, this was the season where Ben was on half salary. So to say that Ben totally depended on the strategy of hope would be wrong at this moment in time.

The pressure created by the half salary as well as taking care of an expectant wife must have pushed Ben to take seriously his coaching students. So he proceeded. He must have been so scared of this new adventure.

**The Power of Pressure**
The only problem Ben had been his focus! Ben thought that his job took precedence over anything and everything. He did not esteem his coaching practice that much. So when his job ended, he just lost the momentum and drive. He gave up. Gave up totally! He no longer coached anybody. He did not want to show up at coaching meetings "without a car"! He gave up because he listened to his fears!

This is exactly how Ben resorted to the strategy of hope, which effectively got him deeper in to adversity. Many people hate adversity. Few people welcome adversity, and these few are not considered to be sane in any way.

> *"Out of tragedy and adversity come great blessings. I shudder to think of what I would have been if I had not gone to prison. Adversity can be God's refining fire".*
> ~Chuck Colson

Interestingly enough, those who love adversity never employ the strategy of hope. It is those who hate adversity, those who are scared of adversity that fully and totally employ the strategy of hope. Yet, I would tell you that adversity has a way of bringing the best out of us. How does that happen?

Well, it is the Law of Pressure at work. Adversity loads pressure on us to such a degree that we have no otherwise than to think. In moments of abundance, a man would choose what to eat. In times of despair, a man would gladly eat a raw frog, I kid you not!

Pressure forces us to think…the very thing that a vast majority of those in the illusion of hope fail to do. Pressure forces us to generate solutions out of seemingly impossible situations. Ben had learnt this when his kid brother was diagnosed with chronic kidney failure.

How Ben and his family were able to spend one thousand dollars every week on dialysis for months on end is a mystery. How they got the money is something else. Yet they did. The pressure of taking care of their loved one made them do things that they would have never done to raise cash. Ben learnt how to wake up at three in the wee hours of the morning and rush his brother to the general hospital, hustling to book a dialysis machine. Adversity had struck the family and they were doing all they could to remain sane.

In his weekly blog, Author Darren Hardy who is also the Publisher of Success Magazine paints a very powerful story that happened several years ago. This was posted on 2nd July 2013:

> Galois was born in France in 1811. During his teens he showed extraordinary brilliance as a mathematician, particularly in algebra. For years he struggled obsessively with a set of algebraic equations.
>
> Then at age 20, he fell in love with a young woman who unfortunately was the fiancée of an artillery officer. When the officer found out about his affections, he challenged Galois to a duel.
>
> Being mightier with his No. 2 pencil (they had those then, right?) than with a pistol, Galois felt certain he'd be killed.
>
> The night before the fateful duel, Galois wrote a summary of all his thoughts on alge-

braic equations. He poured out ideas, some that he had struggled with for years and many new ones that occurred to him in the hours leading up to the duel.

He wrote with great vigor, nonstop all through the night until the final minute before reaching for his dueling weapon.

Galois was right about his firearms abilities: He lost and died.

But he was also right about many of his mathematics ideas. After Galois' death, the notes he compiled on that one night—60 pages of them—were discovered and published. They led to a revolution in higher algebra and had far-reaching consequences in nearly all branches of mathematics. In other words, they rank among the most important ideas in the history of mathematics.

People often wonder what it takes to come up with a big idea.

The reality is your big idea is already inside you but below the surface of consciousness. Over many years, your brain has made billions of observations, collected vast data and built a multitude of key associations.

What does it take to unlock the big breakthrough idea you desire?

Galois' story demonstrates the need for tension, pressure and an urgent deadline to push the ideas out of us. Otherwise the feeling that we have an endless amount of time is insidious and debilitating to the mind. Our attention and thoughts become fractured and dispersed. Our lack of intensity makes it difficult to jolt our brain into high gear, into that higher state of creativity and mental lucidity.

The mind is like much of human behavior. We often don't do what we *want* to do, but we will do the most incredible things when we *have* to.

*If you fall to pieces in a crisis, there wasn't much to you in the first place.* ~ Proverbs 24:10

Darren Hardy couldn't have said it better. "We often don't do what we want to do, but we will do the most incredible things when we have to"

## Forced Lessons vs Chosen Lessons

Some of the purest words you can ever hear are spoken by a man or a woman in adversity. His heart is refined and made tender. His heart is made thoroughly reflective. That is why it is folly to look down and count out a man or a woman going through adversity.

> *"The secret to success is not to try to avoid or get rid of or shrink from your problems; the secret is to grow yourself so that you are bigger than your problem"*
> —T Harv Eker (Secrets of the Millionaire mind)

The truth however is that a great visionary can exert some level of pressure on himself that will make him do things because he has to. That is what adversity does to us in the first place. It accords us the opportunity to really unearth what lies within our greatest reserves. It eliminates lots of 'options' of comfort and forces us to operate in the 'survival mode'. You do not want to stand in the way of a man operating on survival mode. Like a wounded tiger, he's a dangerous man.

The survival mode sometimes suspends beauty and the laws of reason. At survival mode, aesthetics do not matter, just that a life would be preserved. I must add here that it is critical to note that the survival mode should never be deemed to be permanent. Yet at a snapshot of the survival mode, a human being can learn a great lesson, or embrace a virtue, or get a resolve that would always be available for the rest of their lives. They would have otherwise never gotten this.

> *"At survival mode, necessity is the mother of invention. At a visionary mode, dreams are the mother of invention".*

The things that are hitherto considered as the fine things of life, the beauty and comfort of life are normally obliterated by adversity. It goes to show us that these things in real life could be the very impediment to our advancement. At survival mode, necessity is the mother of invention. At a visionary mode, dreams are the mother of invention.

> *"Adversity is the state in which man becomes most easily acquainted with himself being especially free from admirers"*
> –Coach John Wooden

The very first thing that hard times attack when it comes through the door is control. Nothing scares people so much than not being in control. Yet Ben as an executive never really had control of his life, did he? He depended on his employer for salary…the very thing that made him to work. For some reason, his life was centered around the salary. With his salary, he could pay for life's basic needs, and move into the ever expanding middle class. He had the illusion of control. However, as long as his check was being written by someone else, he had no control over it.

That is exactly what adversity came to show Ben. Adversity sent a 'missed call', or 'beeped' when Ben's contract was threatened. He did not hearken. When it finally came to be, albeit two years down the line, Ben did not have the control that he thought he had.

> "Scores and scores of people who have come out of adverse situations have always been grateful people. Grateful, not because of being finally able to come out of the state, but grateful because of the great lessons that they did learn".

If you took a look at Ben's life, the moments of hardship that he has gone through, you will notice that there has been some beauty, lots of beauty out of Ben's ashes. For some reason, that is the paradox of life.

Nelson Mandela, imprisoned for 27 years came out a better man. Once a firebrand who was expelled within one year of High School, he emerged a refined man embracing the 'enemy', working together for the better of their country.

Born deaf and blind, Hellen Keller focused on what she could do with her mind, with the initial help of her teacher, Ann Sullivan. This natural adversity did not put Hellen Keller down, but granted humanity one of the most profound voices of human potential. Maybe Keller would never have been this profound and world class had she not had those impediments in her life. She worked adversity to her advantage.

When Ben finally got stuck proper, it was an opportunity for adversity to draw the best out of him. The biggest problem people have with adversity is that it is never anticipated. The moment it comes, our attitude and disposition denotes that life is not happening, and as a result we live the 'forgotten years' of our lives. We literally stop living and start waiting! We start waiting for things to change, for life to get better!

These 'forgotten years' could otherwise be one of the most valuable years that we can live. It is true that nobody loves to be stressed. Nobody loves or embraces anything that threatens our significance, our certainty and our comfort. Ben might be having no idea that this is a great opportunity in his life. It is an opportunity to review his life. When operating on the 'fast lane', very few people do take some time to really reflect on 'what matters'. Adversity of any form or magnitude is the perfect opportunity for reflection.

Unfortunately, a high percentage of people in adversity are focusing on how to get out of it the whole time it is happening. Apparently, adversity on face value communicates to the world our seeming inadequacies. That's exactly what Ben thought. He thought he was inadequate. When he finally got stuck, he focused more of what he did not have than what he did have. He thought that what he did not have led to his 'stuck-ness'. The result is that Ben ended up reinforcing the stuck situation unconsciously.

Granted, some lessons that adversity hands to us are forced lessons. Such lessons are of unquantifiable value. Scores and scores of people who have come out of adverse situations have always been grateful people. Grateful, not because of being finally able to come out of the state, but grateful because of the great lessons that they did learn.

When Ben was forced to retreat to his village after obtaining is Higher Diploma, it was an adverse situation for him. He fought it all he could. Finally he ended up where never wanted to be—in the village. What would the village help a man who has a Higher Diploma in Information Systems? Of what value did it have? So guess what Ben did? He was restless all the time. He kept refusing his 'fate'. Some people have called it denial. That is the typical anatomy of a forced lesson. Ben refused to do anything constructive with the fear that if he settled, he would be accepting to live in the village all his life. Nothing could be further from the truth.

He refused leadership positions in the local church until it was imposed on him. With that leadership position, Ben actually went about revolutionizing many things in the youth of that church when he finally did get down to it. This adversity revealed what kind of leadership qualities that Ben had. I am sure that without this kind of experience, Ben would hardly know his capacity and potential as a leader, or as a compassionate man, or as a great giver.

---

*"The quality of your life is directly proportional to the amount of uncertainty you can comfortably live with"*
—Anthony Robbins.

---

All these were forced lessons. The situation was cruel. The lessons were not. It is kind of like children. When they are growing up, some of them think that the worst thing ever to happen to them was their parents! They think their parents are eternally restrictive and do not want them to have fun. They think that their parents are obsessed with making life a hell on earth for them. Although you can hardly call that an adversity, the analogy serves us. More than 99% of the kids who thought their parents were the worst thing to ever happen to them later on are more than grateful for the upbringing they were given. Talk of forced lessons.

Life is a seriously objective parent if you will. Life seldom cares about your feelings. I believe life is designed one way or another to bring out the very best out of us. So when we go through adversity at first, we are shaken. However as we move along, we need to start getting the best of the adverse situations of our lives.

Ben's first real adversity is laughable at hindsight. Looking back and connecting the dots, measuring against other forms of adversity that Ben has had, it is laughable that the thing that pained him most was a loss of cassettes of Christian music. These were his hiding place. These are what he retreated to after a day of stress. He hung to them so much and treated them like a baby—with utmost care.

So when this fateful day came, his dad had been cruelly transferred from the city to a smaller town. Ben could not picture that happening. He could not believe that he was destined to leave the city, with no possibility of going back. It so happened that from the packing of the household goods, Ben took special attention to his tapes. He kept them in a special box. His dad was not amused. He grabbed the tapes from Ben and put them in a small hand bag. In the fracas of moving, the hand bag was left behind.

That small adversity shook up Ben so much. Never make a mistake about it, adversity is purely personal! You cannot laugh at somebody else's pain. You cannot compare someone's pain to yours and relegate it to nothingness. At that point in time, the owner of the pain knows it better however small you think it is in your own heart.

**Adversity and Personal Ministry**
Then of course as we move along in life, we tend to 'graduate' to bigger adversities. Hardship and life are one of the truest things you can ever meet. Adversity does not lie. It does not pretend. Life does not lie, neither does it pretend. Life, although lived through hope is very much real. Experiences are real and true. There is however one thing within us that fights what life says or gives, especially in difficult situations.

> *"Never make a mistake about it, adversity is purely personal! You cannot laugh at somebody else's pain. You cannot compare someone's pain to yours and relegate it to nothingness. At that point in time, the owner of the pain knows it better however small you think it is in your own heart".*

When a visionary experiences failure in one area in pursuit of his dreams, he will not simply brush it off but rather learn from it and rise above it.

Life is not static. Life moves on. At the same token, adversity is never static. It is temporary, yet has this overwhelming illusion that it has come to sleep with us forever! The world war ended. The holocaust ended. Famine has come and gone. Small pox, yellow fever and other diseases wasted lives before vaccines were found. In fact the vaccines were obtained from the viruses themselves!

Herein ladies and gentlemen is the greatest of all benefits of hardship—vaccines for viruses. Let me explain: When scientists are coming up with a vaccine against any kind of a virus, they can never have a breakthrough without using samples of the same virus to fight against it. A polio vaccine contains the virus that is responsible for polio. The same applies to any other vaccine that medical science has ever come up with. That should tell us something.

> *"Life is not static. Life moves on! At the same token, adversity is never static. It is temporary, yet has this overwhelming illusion that it has come to sleep with us forever"!*

On the same token, a savior of the people from any kind of slavery is of necessity ruthless with the oppressor yet extremely tender hearted to the oppressed. Do you know how they get tender-hearted towards the oppressed? They feel their pain. They walk where the oppressed walks. They drink the same cup of adversity, and as they do so, their inner witness slowly rises up and starts saying no to the oppression!

I will never forget a message I heard Dr. Mike Murdock share one day titled *'Personal Ministry'*. In that message, Dr. Murdock talks about deliverers feeling the pain of the oppressed. When you all of a sudden start feeling a burden that is unexplained…a fear that grips and paralyzes…all these are not local to you. They are indications that you are a deliverer to someone else somewhere who is experiencing the same thing.

Let's do a quick review on Ben's life. Years after Ben had gone through so much in 'stuckness', he found himself a radio host for the 'Five O'clock Church'. He was the first voice of inspiration that very many mainstream Christians listened to every weekday from 5am. Many of them were inspired by Ben's encouragement. Yet Ben could never have 'delivered them' with his inspiring and comforting messages if he was not going through similar kinds of challenges.

Ben cannot remember the countless times that he was running his program on radio, walking to the studio with the last coin in his pocket, not knowing how he would make it back home. He had left his wife and child without food countless times. His landlord had had several 'discussions' with him about his

> *"Adversity is never for one person. It may be pain for the deliverer, yet when through with him, it forms a beautiful fragrance for others"!*

rent arrears. So when Ben had callers and other listeners requesting for prayers for such things as finances and food and rent, the passionate prayers he made to heaven in his listeners hearing was heartfelt. He personally knew their predicament because his experience was the same. He knew and felt the pain and fears of the countless. Ben knows that he would have never been effective the way he was if he had not gone through the same adversity that he heard his listeners sharing with him.

Countless times his car run out of fuel. Worse, he had to sell of his car to pay for the rent arrears, and yet still he did not have enough bus fare to take him to the doorstep of the radio station. He walked in the wee hours of the morning from the bus station to the radio station on countless occasions. He was a deliverer. Not that he knew that. Life, you see, is understood backwards, but can only be lived forwards. After Ben was through with that 'assignment', then he was able to piece it up together that he was a deliverer. There is no doubt that Ben left an indelible mark with his audience.

---

*"It is in the realm of uncertainty that your passion is found"*
—Anthony Robbins.

---

*Adversity is never for one person. It may be pain for the deliverer, yet when through with him, it forms a beautiful fragrance for others! That is why no hard times are wasted.* At the moment of suffering, the deliverer focuses on nobody else but himself. At the time of living a life in purpose, the deliverer is equipped like no other through hardship!

So next time you see a soul going through unexplained pain and turmoil, the world in its only true yet cruel and weird way, is preparing him to serve others. Life is preparing this mentor to be a fragrance to others. Only a once stuck executive can be an authentic executive coach to others. He knows what pitfalls to avoid, he knows the death grip of fear. He knows how much patience is needed. He has the right words to say to another soul who faces a similar predicament.

That is why it makes a whole lot of sense for Jesus Christ to claim that He is a Savior of the world. Did He walk where we walk? Of course He did. And history attest to this claim. Any independent historian worth his salt with never fail to verify all the accounts about the birth, life, ministry, death and resurrection of Jesus Christ. He is the vaccine against death since He tasted it and conquered it. He is the antidote against pain since He suffered it. He offers respite to the lonely and the lowly since He was both.

*Even God in His own divine nature and wisdom had to use the route of adversity to form His eternal Deliverer. The Savior of the World could not escape adversity. Not that He wanted it…three times or so He earnestly prayed that the hardship He was enduring would pass…that there would be another way.*

That is what we do when misfortune knocks on our doors. We always want another way! Yet such prayers are seldom answered. When adversity hits us and we ask to be delivered from it, hoping for an easier route, we are sometimes met with the deqadest of silences from Heaven. It seems so cruel of the Divine. We might never understand this with our finite minds…but there is purpose, even Divine purpose in misfortune, pain and hardship.

William Wallace was a great deliverer because he suffered the oppression of the people he delivered. When his wife to-be had her throat slit, nobody could fathom his pain.

A young mother lost her daughter in an accident caused by a drunken driver. Nobody can understand her pain. Yet she is now a great deliverer to many mothers who have gone through the same. **Becy Brown** is a great advocate against drunk driving. Her son perished in 1979 through the hands of a drunk driver. She now leads MADD (Mothers Against Drunk Driving)

The man who is the vision bearer of Compassion International, Dr. Wess Stafford, suffered greatly as a missionary kid to his parents in Africa under his teachers. The pain he suffered partly made him such a passionate visionary over injustices.

There is a motivator and clergy called James Robinson. He is a product of rape. Although he is over 50 years old, he has never met his father. James and his wife are great providers to children in Africa.

Ben's vision is to inspire hope and enrich lives worldwide. How did this come about? He had seen a fair share of hopelessness and poverty. Yet he knows deep within his gut that 'there is hope'.

## Surrender and The unquenchable fire inside
At the point of adversity, we can never understand the 'why' even though that is the greatest question on our minds. But I have come to learn that if we can just step aside and reflect on others more than we do on ourselves, we might

> *"At the point of adversity, we can never understand the 'why' even though that is the greatest question on our minds."*

be bound to shorten greatly the hard times that we are facing. The more we focus on ourselves, the more we stay to learn the lesson. The more we put others in focus, the faster we are released to go deliver them!

You see, although all these great men and women did suffer misfortune, some of them unexplainable misfortune, the embers of passion within them were never quenched. In fact it is in their seasons of great uncertainty that their passions were either born or thoroughly fanned aflame!

It is the inner reserves of our hearts that speak bolder and louder. The greatest adversity is not an adversity. The greatest adversity is the silencing of the inner self by an adversity. When a lifelong dream is silenced by an adversity…when passion is eroded by a bad experience, when the dreamer stops dreaming and the visionary gives up on their passion that is the greatest adversity of all!

Now, an interesting thing about harsh conditions, as mentioned earlier, is the taking away of our control. Although great visionaries refuse to give up in the face of difficulty, I do not mean that they are in a total fighting mode all the time. I simply mean that the embers of their desires are never totally put out. They could die down but will never ever be put out.

This brings us to one of the greatest lessons that misfortune forces us to learn—Surrender! Surrender does not mean giving in. It does not mean giving up. It does not mean losing. Surrender simply means accepting. What are we accepting? It is important to accept that we are only human. Surrender allows us to give ourselves the benefit of the doubt. It allows us to acknowledge how feeble we are. It allows us to acknowledge that we are not in total control of our lives. We are not God. We are human, and we are limited to an imperfect world.

The sooner we surrender to the process of adversity, the better! After college, Ben lived in his village, contrary to his dreams. He unknowingly spent over six months living in denial. It is a tough time living in denial while going through hard times. Nobody is happy in denial. And nobody is productive in denial.

Interestingly, when you surrender, you put yourself back in the driver's seat. Surrender says, *"Now that I am here, what is the best possible outcome I can produce? How can I make the best out of this situation while it lasts? Where is the gold in this dark pit? Where is the silver lining in this dark cloud?"*

That kind of thinking is absolute freedom. It happens instantaneously in the mind! A surrendered person is a highly productive person. A surrendered person has a highly absorbent and learning heart. Again, surrender is learnable, and the best teacher of surrender is adversity. There is more joy found in a surrendered person than in one in denial. In fact there is close to zero joy for anyone in denial!

So when Ben stayed in denial all those months, he was a pity to look at. He was a sad long faced fellow. In anything he did, he was unproductive. He was also highly half hearted. This is something you do not want to do to yourself in addition to the adverse situation that you are facing. You need a strong heart. You need a merry heart. These cannot come through denial.

Ben learnt this the hard way. Finally, after months of refutation, Ben totally surrendered to the adverse process. He came out with this philosophy: *"Wherever you go, grow your roots down!"* That is a major lesson to the human soul. It was not surprising that just little over a month after Ben decided to 'grow his roots' that he got called back to the city for an interview on government scholarship.

> *"Surrender does not mean giving in. It does not mean giving up. It does not mean losing. Surrender simply means accepting."*

Ben was over the moon but he also discovered something. *He discovered that hard times had not come into his life to stay, but to teach.* It was temporary. Ben also discovered that he had lost so much time not to adversity, but to denial! He realized that days had passed into weeks while he remained sullen, long faced and sad. He could easily have exchanged those moments and lived fully where he was. That is what surrender could have done to him. The greatest lesson Ben learnt is that the earlier you surrender, the quicker you learn and the earlier you graduate from the adverse situation. *"Nothing we go through is useless!"*

*Remember, surrender however does not mean that what you desired, aspired for and pursued to date has to die! No, surrender does not kill your passion. It does not put off the flames of your pursuits. Surrender does not kill your dreams. Surrender through an adversity firms up your desires.* It brings you the point you say, 'I will do the best I can in the process to having my greatest dreams fulfilled.' What holds a human together is a small spark in their hearts that is wholly connected to hope.

Paradoxically, it is well documented that negative experiences are the greatest catalysts of change. They are the greatest bulwarks of the inner strength. It has been said by an unknown that "the greater they stand the harder they fall!" Revolutions have been made out of adverse situations. Innovations have been made both out of necessity and dreams. The person with a high resilience index has however learnt not only to welcome the forced lessons but also to keep their hopes, dreams and aspirations alive when they come through the dark patches of life. This, I believe is what matters most.

How did Nelson Mandela become so iconic worldwide yet he was a firebrand in his youth? He surrendered. In fact, Mandela was so much surrendered that his cronies thought that 'the old man has become less combative'. They thought he had lost his fire while in prison. He had only surrendered. How did Helen Keller become a world renowned inspiration catalyst? She surrendered to her adversity. How did Ben start experiencing a richer more purposeful and alive life? He surrendered…and grew through the adversity.

In his book Secrets of the Millionaire Mind, T. Harv Eker captures the beauty of adversity in a way that I would have wished I did. That is why I will be quoting him verbatim:

> Poor people will do almost anything to avoid problems. They see a challenge and they run. The irony is that in their quest to make sure they don't have problems, they have the biggest of all…they're broke and miserable. The secret to success, my friends, is not to try to avoid or get rid of or shrink from your problems; the secret is to grow yourself so that you are bigger than any problem
>
> On a scale of 1 to 10, 1 being the lowest, imagine you are a person with a level 2 strength of character and attitude looking at a level 5 problem. Would this problem appear to be big or little? From a level 2 perspective, a level 5 problem would seem like a big problem.
>
> Now imagine you've grown yourself and become a level 8 person. Would the same level 5 problem be a big problem or a little problem? Magically, the identical problem is now a little problem.
>
> Finally, imagine you've really worked hard on yourself and become a level 10 person. Now, is this same level 5 problem a big problem or a little problem? The answer is that it's no problem. It doesn't even register in your brain as a problem. There's no negative energy around it. It's just a normal occurrence to handle, like brushing your teeth or getting dressed.
>
> Note that whether you are rich or poor, playing big or playing small, problems do not go away. If you're breathing, you will always have so called problems or obstacles in your life. Let me make this short and sweet. The size of the problem is never the issue—what matters is the size of you!

I close with this story I credit to the world renowned TD Jakes, the founder of Potters House in Dallas Texas. He vividly portrays the importance of surrender through the story of Jesus Christ on the cross.

In one of the gospels in the Bible, the crucifixion story is painted with a bizarre and cruel incident where the Roman soldiers started breaking the feet of the thieves that had been crucified with Jesus. Why would they do that? You must understand that the Jews were extremely strict with their religious laws. They wanted the three crucified men dead and done away with *before* the Sabbath, so that when they go bury them, they wouldn't be breaking any laws.

So why break their legs? Was it to increase the torture of the crucified so they can die faster? Hardly! When you are on a cross, your breathing is necessitated by the up and down movement of your gut. This is made possible by the fulcrum of your legs. So when I break the bones, I am simply suffocating you in a crude and cruel way. That is what they did for the two thieves that were crucified with Jesus Christ.

However, the most amazing thing is that when they came to Jesus, they *wanted* to break his legs too…but they did not! Why? He was already dead. He had surrendered to the process earlier!

People who have gone through adversity are mostly grateful people. Not to say that they want to go back, but they are grateful for whom they have become –stronger and wiser. They have been tested and now they know how much they can endure. Before the pressure, they did not know they could do what they did. The pressure made them do it.

Another story is told of a basketball star who sprained his right arm. Being a right handed player, he found it challenging to practice even on his own. However, he decided to do something with his situation. He started practicing with his left hand.

It must have been infuriating and frustrating trying to do something new at his age. Persistence and determination was key. He never gave up. To the casual observer, this sportsman was just passing time. It all depends on how we see things. One man sees trouble, another sees opportunity. In the end, what seemed to be a misfortune in the sportsman's life made him even better for he now could dribble with both hands equally well!

Did he want to sprain his hands again? Of course not. Would he wish he never broke his hands in the first place? I don't think so.

---

*"Necessity isn't the mother of invention, your dreams are"*
~ Dutch Sheets

---

# CHAPTER 6:
# The folly and Lessons in Taking shortcuts

*"Life and nature abhor a straight line"*
—Anthony Robbins

The word 'secret' is one of the most used words in online marketing. "The secret to explosive sex", screams one headline. "The secret to becoming a millionaire instantly", beckons another. "The secret to having many followers", another title would offer. No doubt these headlines and titles work. Inherently, we think that what works is hidden from our grasp. So anything branded a 'secret' has a potential of selling.

> *"Lasting success is achieved through processes. When you short circuit the process, you get burnt"!*

It is true that things of value seldom lie on the surface, sometimes we have to dig deep to unearth them. More often than not, what would be diamonds for us is often overshadowed by the never ending quest for the 'hidden secrets'.

That is why natural talents are neglected. That is why many personal gifts are always taken for granted, for they may appear to be as common as table salt. Indeed, it is true that familiarity breeds contempt! You are so gifted in writing that you do not know how valuable it is. To you, it just came naturally and you did not sweat for it. It therefore does not really interest you as diamond would. We tend to think that that which comes either through toiling and sweating or through uncovering a secret is what counts. And so for the most part, we neglect the obvious and follow after the subtle and the grandiose.

**Shortcuts to success**

Next to the word 'secret' is another word 'shortcut'. Well, that word is not used openly. It has been sugar-coated by other words like 'simple', or 'easy', or 'steps'. You would still find people these days using the word 'Instant' to sell. The amazing thing is that many people are attracted to such marketing drives, a host of them.

> "Bullet points, step by step processes that are guaranteed to work overnight, proven shortcuts...
>
> If it was easy, everyone would do it.
>
> Worth noting that surgeons don't sign up for medical school because they're told that there is a simple, easy way to do open heart surgery.
>
> It's not that we're unable to handle complicated problems, it's that we're afraid to try. The Dummies mindset, the get-rich-quick long sales letters, the mechanistic, industrial processes aren't on offer because they're the best we can handle. No, they sell because they promise to reduce our fear.
>
> It will take you less time and less effort to do it the difficult way than it will to buy and try and discard all the shortcuts".
>
> —*Seth Godin (In an article dated 17th August 2013,* http://sethgodin.typepad.com/

seths_blog/2013/08/the-self-defeating-quest-for-simple-and-easy.html)

The very philosophy of secrets and shortcuts is to circumnavigate *time and processes!* The reason as to why many people are attracted to shortcuts and secrets is because they could do without the *process*, but get the *desire*! Unfortunately, life never works that way! Remember that the very nature of adversity is to make us better, wiser, stronger, more involved and more people-centered. Shortcuts and 'secrets' on the other hand would falsely guarantee us success at the absence of our character, the money at the absence of strategies, and the position at the expense of other people! It's called *greed*.

> *"Every negative event contains within it the seed of an equal or greater benefit"*
> —Napoleon Hill

Ben had had his fair share of experiences with applying the shortcuts. He learnt the hard way that shortcuts never work. Now, we are not talking about staying adamant in reinventing the wheel when you could work smarter. Far from it. I honestly think that there is no such a thing as 'the shortcut to success'. Lasting success is achieved through processes. When you short circuit the process, you get burnt!

During his executive days, Ben had learnt to invest some of his finances… although he later on started defaulting, especially with the introduction of the half salary. He had heard of several ways of leveraging other people's money to create wealth. His closest friends back home had already started doing this and it was working for them. The new business scheme was what Ben craved to start working with. It was a perfect shortcut to financial freedom for Ben. He did not have to work, money would work for him. And this, we realize, is the problem with multi-level marketing companies…get rich at the expense of recruits.

## Shortcuts: Laziness, Fear and Greed vs Systems and Processes

There are three great nemeses of success: Laziness, Fear and Greed! To be honest, it is pure laziness to pray for miracles when you have been given options to work with. On the other hand, when someone seeks to amass all at the shortest time possible…they have been bit by the bug of greed. When someone hoards all he knows to be valuable, he is being controlled with this feeling that the more people know, the less successful he becomes. When I am afraid that 'it will disappear before I taste it', that is greed. Unwittingly, this thing controlled Ben so much that he had no idea of what passions it was creating in him.

Sometimes this is so subtle that we do not recognize it. We want instant success. We seek for 'miracles' when we have not understood our mandate. To paraphrase one of the fathers of personal development, *"success is not necessarily what we pursue, but is much more of the person we become. Success must not be pursued, it must instead ensue"*. That is what greed robs people of. You see, I subscribe very highly to God's format namely systems and due processes. If I short-circuit these with greed, yes, I might get rich quickly...however I will greatly miss installing systems that will guarantee my continuous churning out the riches.

> *"The correct way always seems long, hard, tedious and too demanding on us. The easiest way always seems short, quick and extremely comfortable on us"*.

---

*"Always follow the path of most resistance"*
~ Quote

---

We want to get rich quick. We are afraid that the tide will pass us by. Let me say this: anytime you catch yourself thinking that 'I must do this or I miss out'....and you are in a state in which you are not yet ready to get into the fray...watch out that you do not succumb to greed.

I have learnt to take things in stride. Yes, personal development gurus will tell you, "opportunity never knocks twice", but I will tell you this: you only take on an opportunity when you are ready for it. If taking an opportunity has side effects of stress, high blood pressure, getting in debt, losing friends or any other moral wrong...it is absolutely not worth it! The correct way always seems long, hard, tedious and too demanding on us. The easiest way always seems short, quick and extremely comfortable on us.

Every human being that desires to succeed would rather install systems than spend time praying and fasting for miracles....that is my take. If there was a Degree in prayer...Ben has ranked up there with the greatest! When prayer, fasting and dedication are mingled with installed systems in life...you better watch out, a legacy is just about to explode!

The year 2012 started with a huge promise. This to Ben was the year that his most deep-seated desires would be actualized. This was finally the year that he would achieve independence from financial struggle.

His major goals for 2012 were and still are twofold. In fact, everything he had

> *"If something promises you heaven and earth in terms of wealth yet does not require your own daily input in terms of systems and processes, it is a sham and it should be shunned"*.

done so far in the year had revolved around this one theme which is major goal number one--Get back into intimacy with God.

Ben's second major goal was in the year 2012 to open and operate his own E-FOREX Account with a capital base of at least USD 10,000 . This to him was to be one of his several streams of income. He was to do this but still maintain his purpose in life: "To Inspire Hope and Enrich Lives World-wide". Ben knew that he would still need to remain focused in his life purpose which is "To speak a word in season to those who are weary".

Much as setting up that extra stream of income would be a thoroughly daunting task for him, Ben knew that he would never really run away from his mission in life. He believed with all of his heart that his mission on earth is "To treasure the significance of every single person, unleashing each individual's unique purpose by  providing trainings, coaching, writings, motivational talks , giving of self and inspiration to guide people in living legacies.".

**The Anchor of purpose**
There is such a thing as an anchor in life. When a ship is docked at the shore without an anchor, it would drift away from the docking point, slowly drawn out by the waves of the lake or the ocean. That ship would finally get lost.

It is the same thing with our lives. If we lack vision, mission and purpose at the personal level, it is very easy for us to be side-tracked by life's many shining objects that will daily peddle themselves on us. Life's shiny objects are those things that promise you the world in a few days with the least possible input or sweat on your part.

I know I am going ahead of myself, but let me say this: *That if something promises you heaven and earth in terms of wealth yet does not require your own daily input in terms of systems and processes, it is a sham and it should be shunned.*

I know very many people have one major goal in life—to be wealthy. The problem with that set up is that it is not a true heart's desire. It is not a life purpose or vision, to say the least.

Let me illustrate. Many young people's ambition after school is to get a job. I mean their whole lives, efforts, dedication and focus is on being employed, or having a source of income. The only problem with that kind of a focus is that after the job has come, they would then start looking for something else. In other words, they are not in terms with what really matters to them in life. As much as they know they need to, having not defined it condemns them to a life of always seeking not knowing where to seek and worse still, what to find!

It reminds me of the story I heard about a fisherman and a rich man. One day a fisherman was taking a well-needed nap at the shores of the lake after he had caught enough fish to feed his family for the day. A rich man happened to pass by and marveled at this man's inability to seize the opportunity to be rich as it were.

So they had a conversation that went something like this:

Richman: What are you doing?

Fisherman: What does it look like I am doing? I am chewing a sweater! Well of course I am taking a nap.

Richman: Why are you doing that when you could work harder catch more fish?

Fisherman: Wow, I never thought of that. That sounds exciting. OK, tell me more. What do I do after catching more fish?

Richman: What's your problem you lazy man? You sell the fish so you can get some money!

Fisherman: Brilliant idea wise guy…this is exciting. Tell me more please. What do I do when I get some money?

Richman: You will then be able to buy another canoe, employ more people and catch an even greater amount of fish!

Fisherman: Where have you been all my life? I wish you had told me this earlier! You seem to know something that I don't. Please tell me more. What do I do after I have this greater amount of fish?

Richman: [mumbles to himself], "This is more serious than I thought." [Speaks to the fisherman] Don't you see it is obvious? You now have many people working under you, you are their boss, and the sky is the limit! You would then go ahead and form an industry to process the fish and sell it even at an international level!

Fisherman: Brilliant! I knew you were brilliant. Tell me more wise sage…after I have sold the fish to international markets, what next?

Richman: You have more money!

Fisherman: Wow, and then what?

Richman: You become wealthy!

Fisherman: Am excited about this. Then what?

Richman: Then you can be happy!

Fisherman: But I am already happy!

You see, the highest fulfillment of life is relevance and meaning. Relevance and meaning come when people are living their life's purpose. Like I have already said, without a vision or a purpose in life, it is very easy to get side-tracked and join any beckoning shiny object that comes our way. With a life purpose and vision however, one is seriously anchored or tethered. This means that you might move away from the point of the anchor to some distance but will never go past the confines of the length of your anchor.

Given his expertise in Mobile Money Trade Development, Ben had an offer to go back working for the previous company he had worked for to but in a different country. That was some time back in 2011, the third quarter of the year. At that time, his vision, purpose and mission in life were coalescing so much to fruition. He was becoming a much sought-after speaker. He immediately turned that offer down ostensibly because of the way he was treated in the previous assignment.

I am saying that to bring the point of anchoring home. Sometimes, one might have to do something way outside of your calling or purpose as a 'necessary evil'. In his situation, Ben had this opportunity beckoning. He also had this lucrative opportunity to turn his fortunes around by being close to the 'kitchen' that cooked hard currencies in E-FOREX Trading, a company that he had just been introduced to. He thought in all due honesty, that he could take the E-FOREX route but still end up 'Designing Legacies' as is the tag of his company 'Life Signatures'.

You see, sometimes in life, you could take a tangent that openly veers off of the your life purpose for the reason of coming back to it well equipped, either with finances, experience, materials, or networks of people that will help you champion your main vision for the rest of your life.

In fact, Ben was so focused on 'Designing Legacies' that he remember at one point in time, the local business in the country that was operating the E-FOREX Business literally asked him: *"What would it take for us to use your tagline 'Designing Legacies!'"*

So in his pursuit of financial wealth through the E-FOREX Market, Ben was glad that his guiding principle has always remained attached to his life purpose. As mentioned earlier, his life that year had two major themes. By all indications, he was on course on both fronts. Ben had taken the month of

January 2012 off from all his activities including writing, blogging, social media, coaching, mentoring and speaking to focus on getting a general direction for the rest of the year.

As such, he designed an anchor through this separation that was premised on five fronts. These are:

- To Reconnect with God in deep intimacy and build a lifestyle and altar of prayer
- To introduce one more stream of income in his life through E-FOREX Trading online
- To become a Published Author
- To become a Certified and anointed Life Coach
- To run two Marathons

At this point in life, Ben was on course on all of these points save one, the E-FOREX Trading online. As pertains reconnecting with God and building a lifestyle and altar of prayer, it was instituted and grew big. Not only did he have his own prayer altar, Ben was also privileged to be the voice of inspiration and prayer in one of the mainstream Christian stations in the country every morning at five O'clock.

As concerns becoming a published author, he had already finished a manuscript for his first ever written book, 'Permission For Greatness… bridging the gap between school and relevance'. Ben had already been in touch with his publisher as far as that work is concerned and was sure of being published by the close of the year.

As far as becoming a Certified Life Coach is concerned, Ben was still on course. He had been life-coaching for years and had really desired to become certified, since his scope is the world, starting with East and Central Africa. He had been in communication with the relevant bodies that he wants to be affiliated with as far as this is concerned and was sure that by the close of the year, it will be a reality.

The previous year had been a very interesting one in his life. It was the first year in his stay in the foreign country that Ben was completely broke and stuck; having acrimoniously ended his expatriate consulting on Mobile Money with the firm he was working with. It is the same year that his wife and first born of three days were detained in hospital due to unsettled bills. Ben had set aside enough money to pay for a normal delivery. But due to the baby's size the doctor had to do a C-section, a procedure that more than doubled the hospital bill.

## Following the trail

2012 was also the year where the concept of 'My Jog To Success' an ever upcoming project was birthed. This project came out of a decision Ben took at the height of the limbo in his life to 'do anything' but sit at home and whine. The 'anything' for this matter was jogging.

Taking action opened him up to several opportunities. It is amazing how in life, even the most unlikely and remotest things are connected. Ben's jogging exercise connected him to a popular group of 400 visionaries in the city that met once a month. He met several previous acquaintances of the past years, men who were strategically placed for business growth.

Sarah worked for Private Sector Foundation in a senior position. Having attended one of Ben's passionate lectures, she vowed to help him get more exposure at bigger events.

At that meeting, she also informed Ben that one of his former coaching clients was launching a book, and that he was invited to attend. He gleefully did that and met other prominent authors including a key Educationist of whom he had a very interesting discussion about his feelings on the focus of education. Ben asked him about his opinion on his upcoming book, 'Permission For Greatness'. He also spoke with so much passion about the E-FOREX Market that one attendant at the Book launch, unbeknown to Ben, was a member of the 400 visionaries. Their Forum was looking for someone to interview that coming week on Principles of Investment, and so this participant immediately forwarded Ben, to the CEO of the Forum.

In short, Ben got a slot to be interviewed on the Forum under the rightful introduction of 'the man who introduced Mobile Money to the country', and his interviewer was a popular media personality. To date, both the Forum CEO and the Media personality have no idea that Ben did not have transportation to get to the Forum and that he had given up completely until his wife encouraged him to make one phone call to a new friend and ask for help… just one hour before the function! Talk about being stuck!

After Ben was interviewed at the Forum, he was also invited to be the Keynote Speaker at the next meeting under his pet subject, "Personal Branding". Ben reckons that he did a pathetic job by his standards. He was incoherent and uncoordinated. He read his notes from a bunch of papers; the information was not coming from his heart or head. Every time he sees his DVD for that day, he feels ashamed and embarrassed.

Yet that did not stop him from being introduced to a popular TV Breakfast show to be interviewed by the same popular media personality on a subject that he forgets. From there on Ben was interviewed on another TV station on several occasions focusing mostly on inspiration. He was also interviewed on three more radio stations in a space of one month! His message on human potential never changed in all these cases. So as you can see, that was a very interesting year for Ben.

Yet like I have said previously, 'looks can be very deceiving'. Am sure either the attendees at the Forum, the viewers on TV stations as well as the listeners on those radio stations must have envied Ben greatly. He was 'looking good' but I was far from being really 'good'. He looked good, but was broke.

> "All through life, people long for and look for success. Some look for the shortest way to it, others look for the easiest way to it. Some wait for it to come to them, others go find it. Some use smart ways to achieve it; others use traditionally prescribed methods to attain it. Some connive and defraud to attain it; some use their raw and natural talents to obtain it. Some attain it and lose it; some guarantee its repetition through building processes and systems".

So 2012 was a year with double blessings for Ben. It was the year of their wedding and also the birth of their first child. It is also that self same year that he tested life in using public transport, after surrendering the company cars that he was previously driving. It is also in year that Ben benefited indirectly from the E-FOREX Business by owning his own vehicle.

I took lots of joy and pride riding in that car with his bride and son to his country home to visit his parents. Not that he had not driven home in a car before; he had done that with the company vehicles previously. This however, was different: His own car, his own bride, and his own son. Some would say, "The man has arrived!"

When this was happening, Ben had seen tremendous unparallel success with the E-FOREX Business and was now under the complete illusion that the following year would literally explode in his life. This illusion has caused many people to throw away best practices in business and completely banked on the 'mirage of success'.

All through life, people long for and look for success. Some look for the shortest way to it, others look for the easiest way to it. Some wait for it to come to them, others go find it. Some use smart ways to achieve it; others use traditionally prescribed methods to attain it. Some connive and defraud to attain it; some use their raw and natural talents to obtain it. Some attain it and lose it; some guarantee its repetition through building processes and systems.

So let us rewind this story a little bit to show how Ben really got hooked to this shortcut. Using a colleague's reference and the information he already had about the success of the Forex market from the members of his family, Ben was ready to jump on board. One of the Directors of a newly formed company happened to occupy the house in which his former colleague had just vacated. He had been informed about Ben's desire to join the trade, so he paid Ben a visit.

After Ben's interaction with this man, Ben was sold! Ben saw how the system worked. In fact, one thing that really resonated with him was that he wanted to help people with their financial education. In fact, later on, Ben would tell people that he provided the 'what' (information), and this company provided the 'how' (mechanics) of financial freedom!

The Forex Market is legitimate across the globe. You could take classes and learn how to be a Forex Trader. Every day, currencies are traded close to three trillion US Dollars on the currencies market. It is a vast market. However, it is a capital intensive business, needing deep pockets to operate.

So what did this company do? They 'borrowed' money from people using contracts prepared by a Lawyer. They promised to give people a certain percentage of their 'investments' every month, and that in a period of just six months, they would have recouped their initial investment. The deal sounded so real and so lucrative. For good measure, the company told the people not to take their word for it, but to also do their own research. The clients were encouraged not to rush but to be patient before they invest.

However, who wants to be patient and be by-passed by this wonderful opportunity? Immediately Ben heard that pitch, he started scratching his head for finances. Ben knew that if only he could get an initial amount of money and invested…he would not need to worry about paying his monthly rent. That would be a thing of the past.

Ben looked at this wonderful opportunity with so much hunger and desire! God must have sent these guys! He needed a way of getting residual income. He needed a way for money to work for him and not the other way round, and voila! The solution was here. Ben was convinced that this was of God.

When he could not raise the initial capital, Ben got to learn from this company that if he introduced someone, he would earn 5% of their initial capital investment! Ben saw his chance and got active, recruiting everyone who cared to listen. How else do you think Ben ended up at the TV and Radio stations? It is the passion that he exuded while pitching for the Forex Trade that got the attention. Ben was so pure hearted at this and knew that he would help many people.

Now, guess who would be the first people that you would talk to when you strike gold? Of course your family and friends! Ben rounded them up so hard that he started earning his commissions. His wife joined the bandwagon and started talking to her circles of influence as well. She was so passionate about this that she converted the entire crew that was helping her at the delivery of her first born son! It was incredible! Life was on the upswing again. Our stuck executive was no longer stuck. He was now cruising.

Towards the end of the year, Ben had benefited indirectly from the company. He had shown great interest in learning the mechanics that he not only learnt, but also started teaching the clientele of the company at a fee! He had organized the classes to make it mandatory that anybody wishing to learn the mechanics would first of all take coaching classes that Ben organized.

Then came the car. This was the pinnacle of it all. Ben was now convinced that all was working well...and then it happened! One director started confiding in Ben that all was not well. A red flag right there. He told Ben that there was not only misunderstanding, but also misappropriation of funds at the company. Heads in the cloud and blind to the truth, Ben did not heed that red flag. After Christmas, as the clients were waiting for their dividends, the rude shock came that the company had suffered a loss...and that It would need another three months to recover.

The three months came and went...and with them, Ben was slowly going back to those old days of being broke and stuck...this time round with the addition of guilt as he had invited very many people to be 'partakers' of this venture. Life must be playing a very bad game on Ben. When people started demanding their pay, and some a total refund of their investments, the directors ran out of stories and excuses and quickly became unavailable.

Let us flash forward to Thursday 19th July 2012. The following words were written by Ben in his diary:

> It is a few minutes past five a.m. I am supposed to be at the radio station leading the prayer altar till six a.m. I cannot make it since I am exhausted and unprepared and

'dry'. It is also approximately ten hours since I was released from detention at Central Police Station. The charge preferred against me is "Obtaining Money by Fraud". The police picked me up from my house at around four thirty p.m. on Monday the 16th July 2012. I was released on police bond and now I have to report back to Central Police Station on 25th July 2012 about this case.

The complainant is one of the clients of the Investments Company that has been dealing with the E-FOREX Business in the country since early 2011. I joined this company because I loved their 'vision'. In the spirit of staying relevant and anchored, I offered to integrate my coaching classes together with E-FOREX Classes that the company sought to offer…and so there I am, 36 Hours behind bars.

Looking back to January 2012, I can see the irony. After 30 days of preparing and strategizing for the year, I really felt God was speaking to us as a family is that in 2012, we would be "lifted up from obscurity to levels of relevance and prominence". That word resonated strongly in my heart and spirit. I have it embedded on the desktop of my computer, and I see it every single day when I turn it computer on.

That can be a very ironical and even cynical statement given the circumstances that I find myself in, seven months down the line in 2012. Yet again, that statement can still hold lots of water in it. I mean, how obscure can one get? From 'the man who introduced Mobile Money' to a suspect who is being stripped of his wedding ring by inmates at CPS, thoroughly being ransacked for any valuables he could be carrying up to his inner wears—a welcome party to life behind bars!

Now that is as obscure as it gets, given that the police cells are underground the central police station! Yet it gives me hope that prominence and relevance are right ahead, beckoning me. It is amazing how a genuine cause to enrich lives and be part of the E-FOREX Trading handed me 36 hours in the coolers. It is amazing that that is a stark contrast in reality to what I envisioned for my life at the beginning of the year.

As I write, all the three Directors of the company are at large, moving from one house to another, evading their clients' calls. As for me, I will not run. I will stay put. I will pay the price. I will take the full responsibility of my ill-informed action. My heart was pure. My passion to help was unbridled. My excitement about the prospects was unparalleled. My eloquence to new clients was impeccable. I never saw gray areas. I only saw black and white. Like many clients who have lost thousands of dollars, I was convinced that this was a way of working smarter rather than working hard. Now I know better.

To be fairly honest, we cannot blame Ben for taking this route. The man had an opportunity and literally jumped onto it. In fact, you might want to give him a standing ovation for that. However, in the end, it did not work! That is exactly what shortcuts do. They *do not* work. When you are through with them, for the most part you have veered off your mandate, you are laden with guilt, and you are a pale shadow of who you were before you ventured!

That is why it is critically important for us to know how to define and recognize any shortcut to success. In this present age of information, you need subtility indentify a shortcut. However, from Ben's story we are able to learn this and that about how to avoid shortcuts in our quest to get unstuck or in our bid to be successful.

**Recognizing a Shortcut: 7 Yardsticks**
At the core of a success story, the main character is fully involved and fully engaged. He is in total control of all his resources that he is channeling towards success. *If somebody is prescribing to you a formula for success in which your involvement and control does not matter, you ought to shun it. It is especially more dangerous if you will bear all the consequences of failure per chance the prescription of success does not work. It simply means you are being used.*

**Secondly** if anything or anyone prescribes to you a formula for success that is purely monetary, you need to think twice. In our case, our stuck executive obviously needed money. Yet there are other things that he could focus on and not just money.

This is a crucial and paradoxical point. Yes, Ben worked in convincing people to join the trade. Yes, he worked in training the clientele of that organization. The overall question however still goes back to the issue of control. Were the clients in control of their money? No they were not!

> *"I have always been the opposite of a paranoid. I operate as if everyone is part of a plot to enhance my well-being"*
> —Stan Dale

**Thirdly**, a shortcut is anything that promises you your wildest dreams ever over a record time! True, there are things that we can do that can shorten the process of acquiring our desires. However, these things have already passed test number two above. For example, Goal Setting is not only a success principle, but also a divine strategy for making us better in addition to acquiring what we desired to become or have.

If, by the end of the process you are involving yourself in you do not get better as a human being in terms of virtues, beliefs, character and vision, eventually the tangible gains you are getting come to a halt. The

> *"At the core of a success story, the main character is fully involved and fully engaged. He is in total control of all his resources that he is channeling towards success. If somebody is prescribing to you a formula for success in which your involvement and control does not matter, you ought to shun it".*

tangible gains deteriorate and ultimately grow wings and fly away, leaving you as empty as a vacuum.

**Fourthly**, God has already said that 'my people perish for lack of knowledge'. It is instrumental to note that one of the greatest investors of the present world has said that he would never invest in anything that he does not understand. The same should apply to all of us. Knowledge does not mean mental assent. Knowledge means intimate understanding. If you do not have an intimate understanding of the process that you are undertaking, especially if it is being conducted by somebody else…and you also do not have an intimate understanding of that person, you are short-cutting.

> "The blessing of the Lord makes a person rich, and he adds no sorrow with it"
> –King Solomon (Proverbs 10:22)

**Fifthly**, we have already said that anybody without a vision is bound to fail. Vision is extremely critical. Vision should serve others more than it serves self. Ben joined this organization that had activities going but they lacked vision. Vision is able to sustain something through thick and thin because it has already anticipated the tough and tumble. If you are joining a process just to sort you out on one aspect, and that project lacks vision, you might be short-cutting. *One thing about shortcuts is that they serve the present moment so accurately sufficient that they give an illusion of perfection over the coming age of the future.* So you might be basing your decision on the bells and whistles of the now… and forget to check the firmness of the project over a long period of time. Vision is not for tomorrow. Vision is for generations. If they do not have a vision, they are short-cutting.

**Sixth**, many people shun the advice of the legal bodies around. People are so desperate to make a kill in the shortest time possible that they will do everything but check with the local authorities. If the project you are involving yourself with does not have any legislation from the government of the day, it means that you have no security incase anything goes wrong. You cannot afford to do that.

A simple enquiry would help unearth the answer. Let me say that lawyers are not necessarily the people to ask. Lawyers can defend anything on the face of the earth. That is why there will always be defense lawyers no matter how obvious a case is. In fact as this is being written, a case in the United States in which a white man who was armed killed 'in self defense' a black young man has raised a tumult. That white man was set free! If you want to find out about legislation of a project, a process or a business, you ask a governmental body and not a lawyer. The company Ben joined hired an advocate of the high court to help 'legalize' their contracts. No governmental body was involved in the process.

**Lastly**, a shortcut can be seen from miles ahead if it offers to cover all your costs and losses. Only God Almighty has the capacity to do that. This is life and in the dance of life, it takes two to tango. When you enter into a relationship of any kind and the other party promises to cover all the negatives that the relationship will suffer…you are being enticed. Many people love to have a normal heart beat. We do not want our hearts to race because we are afraid to fail, or because we are incurring losses. That is why when someone or a company promises to bear all the losses, many people welcome the idea. Well, from Ben's experience, that should be a red flag right there.

In a nutshell, the following things will help us minimize our natural tendencies to take shortcuts in life:

**Values:** Knowing your top 10 values that you cherish in life (both in your life and in the lives of others)
**Life Purpose:** Knowing why you are here on earth
**Life Goals:** Creating a strategic plan for your life

---

*"No man ever became great or good except through many and great mistakes"*
—William E. Gladstone, former Prime Minister of Great Britain

---

When all is said and done, in the spirit of getting unstuck, we cannot say that Ben lost when he took the shortcut. Ben learnt quite a lot. The above seven points are a testimony of the same. Shortcuts will never get us where we want….when we take them, we do not lose…we just learn the hard way!

# CHAPTER 7:
# The Abundance of Options

*"Capacity is defined as the belief that you already have within you all that you want, need, and choose. Capacity is not just the recognition that you are standing on top of a treasure chest of gold. It is knowing that you are the treasure chest. The gold is inside you, waiting to be invested"*

—Kim George

What we have here in Ben's story is what most people consider as a misfortune. The human soul never likes trouble. The human soul loves comfort and ease. The paradox is that comfort and ease never create the highest form of human satisfaction—to matter.

> *"Notice though that it is not the reality that is creating the belief. It is the illusion communicated from the reality that easily forms a belief. The truth is that you have two options. You can accept the reality and reject the illusion or you can believe the illusion together with the reality".*

Everybody in a pressurized circumstance would want to get out soonest. This is completely sane. It is also completely human to want to solve a situation as quickly as possible. We all do not want hardship to linger on one more day. There is only one man in historical records who wanted adversity one more night…the Ancient King of Egypt, the Pharaoh when asked by the 'Prince of Egypt' when he wanted the hoards of frogs to disappear. Pharaoh said, "Tomorrow!"

My take however is that a stuck situation is like a gold mine to a human soul…if we only noticed. We should also note that one crisis is always different from the previous and the next. Our skills in handling a crisis would go a mighty long way in making us resilient. It would also go a long way in making us the messengers of hope to those who are where we used to be. Pressure can be good, if we look at it with a different set of eyes. Consider how many records have been broken because of pressure. Consider how many inventions have been made throughout human history purely from adversity!

**Mental Games: Interpretations of Illusions and Realities**
For good measure, sometimes all the obstacles that we see in hardship are mostly mental. Why would we call a 'stuck' situation to be adverse? It could be because we inherently *think* that there are absolutely no options, at least from our own internal selves! It is because we consider ourselves helpless and powerless in the wake of what we are going through.

This is one of the major reasons as to why people resort only to hoping and praying and waiting! Someone somewhere has told us that it cannot be done and there are no options. We hear that and accept it at face value without a question. We become paralyzed by an illusion, like that stallion I saw chained on a 500g plastic chair on social media!

For the record, a setback is not a stuck situation; it simply is life giving us feedback. Tony Robbins says that life and nature abhor a straight line. I have never seen a life without adversity. It happens to all of us, even to the Royals. We are all human prone to trouble as we have already seen in the first chapter of this book.

Being stuck can simply be the function of the mind. It can also be the function of a belief. Yes, the physical *reality* you are in at the moment will indicate otherwise. The *reality* will communicate that there is no money. The *illusion* will say that your better days have long gone.

The *reality* will say that the divorce is real…and the *illusion* will add that you will never ever enjoy the thrills of marriage, a family and a home. The *reality* will say that you have flanked the papers today, and the *illusion* will spice that message up just a little bit to indicate that you will never ever make it in life. The *reality* will tell you that you are a lousy speaker from the feedback of the audience and the *illusion* will amplify the message that you were never 'called' to speak.

**The Power of Delusions**
The *reality* will tell you without lying that the sales have not come in the past three months and the *illusion* will add that you will never ever succeed. **Notice though that it is not the reality that is creating the belief. It is the illusion communicated from the reality that easily forms a belief.** The truth is that you have two options. You can accept the reality and reject the illusion or you can believe the illusion together with the reality.

Do you want to know the master key in this situation? It is little T-word. Both the reality and the illusion are temporary! You should never forget this.

> Nick Sitzman was a strong, healthy, and ambitious young railroad yardman. He had a reputation as a diligent hard worker and had a loving wife and two children and many friends.
>
> One midsummer day, the train crews were informed that they could quit an hour early in honor of the foreman's birthday. While performing one last check on some of the railroad cars, Nick was accidentally locked in a refrigerator boxcar. When he realized that the rest of the workmen had left the site, Nick began to panic.
>
> He banged and shouted until his fists were bloody and his voice was hoarse, but no one heard him. With his knowledge of "the numbers and the facts", he predicted the temperature to be zero degrees. Nick's thought was, 'If I can't get out, I'll freeze to death in here. Wanting to let his wife and family know exactly what had happened to him, Nick found a knife and began to etch words on the wooden floor. He wrote, "It's so cold, my body is getting numb. If I could just go to sleep. These may be my last words"

The next morning, the crews slid open the heavy doors of the boxcar and found Nick dead. An Autopsy revealed that every physical sign of his body indicated he had frozen to death. And yet the refrigeration unit of the car was inoperative, and the temperature inside indicated 55 degrees Fahrenheit. Nick had killed himself by the power of his own thoughts.

–From Jack Canfield's Success Principles.

You will agree with me that the reality is seen through the lens of the mind. A whole generation can be held captive by believing an illusion…which we have already seen that at best, it is temporary. The biggest illusion in the moments of crisis is the lie that there is nothing you can do…that there are no options available.

Think of how many other barriers have turned out to be only mental obstacles:

**The sound barrier**: Pilots didn't think it was possible to fly faster than 768 miles an hour (the speed of sound at sea level). Then Chuck Yeager officially broke the sound barrier on October 14, 1947.

**The four-minute mile**: Runners didn't think it was possible to run a mile in less than four minutes. Then, in 1954, Roger Bannister ran it in 3:59.4.

**The two-hour marathon:** Endurance athletes didn't think it was possible to run a marathon in less than two hours. Now several athletes are on the verge of breaking Geoffrey Mutai's world-record of 2:03.02.

I could also mention the high jump…there was a mental limit on it. Until a certain athlete came up with the back-flip style, now called the '*Fosbury Flop*'. Richard Douglas Fosbury 'flopped' all the way to setting the world record in High Jump in the 1968 Olympics. The truth is Fosbury *presented himself with an alternative option* after the whole world had declared that it was impossible to do a high jump of greater than two meters! Almost all high jumpers to date have resorted to the *Forsbury Flop*…and it works!

But this is what we see all around the world and specifically in individual's lives. Many people robbing themselves of legacies because of mental blocks, delusions, fear, the dark side of hope, and the illusion that there are no options whatsoever!

---

> *"Nobody— not your boss, job, house, car, husband, wife, or dog—can add to your Capacity. They can provide support as you expand your Capacity, but they can never complete you or give you more Capacity".*

―Kim George

**Taking Action**
*There has never and never will there be in this fallen world, such a thing as a perfect moment to take action.* Certainly, when we are facing hardship, we inherently tend to think that we should be given a break…and so we do nothing… until the imperfect moment passes on.

I am willing to bet that the times of least inspired activity in our lives are found in the moments of adversity. Mostly it is because we are so crippled by this debilitating fear that just emasculates us. I do not think there is a human being who has never felt this kind of disabling fear. We all have. However, courage is taking action in spite of the fear. I am not being hard on you when I say that you need to take action in the moments of adversity. I am not being sadistic, uncaring and inconsiderate.

I am simply saying that the card we play of non action in the moment of difficulty is the worst card we can pull out at any time. The only place where we can resort to non action is when our civil liberties have been taken away by another person. It is only when we have absolutely no control; we are confined and constrained that we can resort to non action. Even then, men and women have learnt that there is still something that they can do.

I read the story of Captain Gerald Coffee who was an American pilot in during the Vietnam War. He spent more than seven good years as a prisoner of war. He was mistreated, tortured, and malnourished and endured so much that we cannot even begin to fathom and compare with some of our own adversities. Granted, it is never prudent to compare adversities, since hearts are different, lives are different and so are experiences.

*"Each heart knows its own bitterness and no one else can fully share its joy"* —Proverbs 14:10

Captain Coffee however learnt that he had options he could work with even in the solitary confinement that he was subjected to. It is well documented that solitary confinement can cause people to run mad. However, Captain Coffee asked himself this question: *"How can I use this experience to my advantage?"* In his book, The Success Principles, Jack Canfield picks up the story as follows:

> He told me that he decided to see it as an opportunity rather than a tragedy—an opportunity to get to know both himself and God—the only two beings he'd be spending time with—better.
>
> Captain Coffee spent many hours each day reviewing every interaction he had ever

had with anyone in his life. Slowly he began to see the patterns of what had worked and what hadn't worked in his life. Over time, he slowly psychoanalyzed himself. Eventually he came to totally know himself at the deepest levels. He fully accepted every aspect of his being, developed a profound sense of compassion for himself and of humanity and came to fully understand his true nature. As a result, he is one of the wisest, humble and peaceful men I have ever met. He literally radiates love and spirituality. Though he admits that he would never want to have to do it again, he also says that he would not trade his experience as a prisoner of war for anything, for it has made him who he is today—a deeply spiritual and happy family man, a successful author, and one of the most moving inspirational speakers you could ever hope to hear.

—Jack Canfield, The Success Principles: How to get from where you are to where you want to be.

I cannot say it enough: There are always options to work with… and in several cases, there is always an abundance of options.

## Options are always Hidden Goldmines

If we begun to examine Ben's abundance of options, you might be shocked at what goldmine this man was sitting on. *The issue is not that there are no options; the issue is that we are mostly plagued by illusions and fear.* Like already seen, we 'wait' instead of living. We 'hope', instead of taking action. Many people have had their adversities but a vast majority of them cannot say together with Captain Gerald Coffee that they 'would not trade their experience in adversity for anything'. Why is that?

*It is because when adversity comes, we stop living and start wishing.* Now, let us realize that that is one of the most natural responses you can have when a hardship comes. It is a self-preservation mechanism. As much as it is natural, this technique does not help us in rebuilding our resilience index.

Another major reason as to why we do not see the abundance of options in adversity is that we have learnt over our lifetime to ascribe value to experiences differently. We normally put an immediate or monetary worth on our options.

Sometimes, getting out of the hardship is not necessarily the answer. Sometimes, when we start experiencing different things in life, we might as well need to accept the situation. I have heard people talking of accepting 'new normals'. I can understand that phrase because as we have already seen, life has a permanence called change. The terminology of 'new normals' would certainly put a time aspect to a difficult patch in our lives. That phrase would spell to us that the hardship is here to linger a while…yet that is hardly what we want to hear. That is why we operate purely on what monetary or immediate value the options we have will bring. We think we have no option because from the choices we have, there is no immediate or monetary gain coming in to get us out of the limbo.

> *"Take the first step in faith. You don't have to see the whole staircase. Just take the first step".*
> –Dr. Martin Luther King Jr, Legendary civil rights leader.

If an option that we are taking is not getting us out of the hardship immediately, we brush it aside. We consider it as useless. That is why you would always hear this statement: *"Yeah, but where is the money?"* I have to warn you beforehand that the abundance of options available to us in moments of adversity seldom will give us immediate monetary gain. In fact, the abundance of options we have in constrained situations in life will always be to focus on the intangibles of life… things like vision, values, mission, and purpose.

Let me ask you a question. What is the best time to shop for a car? Now, this is not a trick question. It is an important Life Signatures question. What is the best time to shop for nice sofa sets and curtains? Let me tell you when: The best time to shop for stuff is when you have no dime in the pocket! You know why? You tend to be very objective and you tend to have lots of time and patience to get the best at the perfect price. In a nutshell, that is why Goal Setting is important. We never set goals when we can acquire them the next minute!

Woe to you if you had MONEY enough to purchase your type of car…and you have not taken time to shop around. I assure you that from the first car dealership you enter, you will drive away with a vehicle. Then later on after the 'itch' you had to get that vehicle has been satisfied, you will start realizing that you could have waited longer, you could have shopped more, you could have compared prizes more…you could have gotten a better deal! Some people call it 'buyer's remorse'.

**The Money Question**
Have you ever had this statement: "I wish I had the money…I would…" The flip side of my earlier question is this. Very many people are hand-cuffed in the illusion that without cash, they can do nothing. So you do not find people shopping for where they want to go or what they want to own…because they have no cash right now. You find a visionary like Ben not writing a book…'because I have no cash to publish it'. Isn't that just pretty myopic?

Honestly speaking...the many things that we abdicate doing, do they really need cash? How much cash do I need to finish a manuscript? How much cash do I need to put a magazine together before it is published? How much cash do you need to do something about that thing that you are passionate about right now? In most cases, hardly a dime!

---

*"Waiting is not the absence of movement or activity, waiting is a force"*
— Dr. Mike Murdock

---

Yes, in the end, I will need the cash for my website, my new books, and all the projects of Life Signatures...but that is just that...in the end. Which tells you that we can do something right now with whatever is available within us... even when there are no visible funds to bring the project to completion.

Look at it this way. There is a big passionate visionary, whose vision is to finance all the 'stalled' projects. All he wants is to see the passion and the project...and inject in the finances. Pray tell me...do you think he will finance whatever vision is in your head? Hardly! Do you think he will finance the invisible project? However passionate you are about it, if you have not done what you are in control of right now, you will not be in luck. In fact, if he was financing my book, he will very well like to read my manuscript. Now...where is that manuscript? Do not tell me you don't have it since you did not know where money to print it will come from! Break those illusionary handcuffs off of you that tell you can do nothing until cash shows up! Cash hardly shows up where there is nothing!

I hope we understand the gist of this message. Stop sitting on your laurels because you do not see the end of your project right now. You are not God Almighty! He's the only One able to see the end from before the beginning from all dimensions. Our calling is to take charge of what is in our domain right now. Do not say you cannot sing because you do not have money. Money does not make your voice smooth...practice does!

It is difficult to talk about legacies without touching that subject of money . It takes provision to finance a visionary's dreams. Yet I have come to realize that money is simply the grease, the oil that makes the machinery synergize. Without cash, it is impossible to bring the vision to fruition. Yet, the cash is not paramount! Without the vision, forget about the cash! What do you need the cash for?

---

*"For every failure, there's an alternative course of action. You just have to find it. When you come to a roadblock, take a detour"*

–Mary Kay Ash.

All visionaries should come to that place where they have no dime to finance their vision. In fact, very few visionaries really start out with all the pieces of the puzzle in place. Much as it would be okay to have everything in place for our dreams and visions, I prefer that we only have the seeds, the concept of the dream. This way, we can do all there is to do that is within our control for the sake of the vision. In fact, how badly are we passionate about the dream? It will show when we keep on believing despite the seeming 'lack' of money.

Listen, the other way of spelling money is V-A-L-U-E. All you have at the moment without the money, is to add concept after concept to the dream thus building multiple VALUE. Then when the money comes (It shall surely come, I tell you), you will then move with utmost speed. Remember the Chinese bamboo that is watered for four years even before it sprouts from the ground then shoots up to 45 Meters High in two months? That is the VALUE I am talking about.

*The worth of an individual or a vision is not the amount of money in the petty cash box right now.* Especially when we find ourselves in a hardship, we need this revelation deep in our hearts. It is very easy to have our self esteem hit an all time low during difficult patches of our lives. We mostly attach our worth to our well-being…which in turn has our self confidence attached to it.

This statement is deep and worthy of a retake. *My worth is not necessarily my money…that can get lost tomorrow…but can also be earned from my worth anytime.* That is why misplaced elements will always shoot at you when you exude passion about your dream, "Yeah, but where is the money?" They are gauging the progress of your dream and vision with how much money you have to throw around. Just because there could be no physical cash to show off your efforts right now does not mean you abandon the vision to something that brings in quick cash. There is nothing like quick cash. It is a fantasy. Real steady flowing income more or less follows value. I do not necessarily need cash to build value do I?

**The Setback-Comeback Gap**
This brings me to this point. Ben is our stuck executive mostly because he was focusing on what will get him out of the hardship immediately. He also was focusing on that which would give him monetary gain instantly. When he could not find those things readily available, he became discouraged, gave up and essentially reinforced his stuck state! Now let me be quick to add this: It is pretty much OK to look for an option that will get you out of a crisis faster.

It is OK to look for an option that will generate the necessary finances you will need to unstuck you. However, that is not the only option available…so if that option is not immediately apparent, it does not mean you get emasculated by doing nothing. Someone has said that life is what happens when we are busy making other plans. It is the 'in between transition' moments that have time and time again proved to be more valuable than options for direct cash and instant freedom from crisis.

I have to be careful here. I am not saying that we should look forward to one more night with the frogs like Pharaoh. When a loved one is diagnosed with cancer, it would be inhuman of me to insist that you should stay in that state a little longer ostensibly to 'learn a lesson'. That is not what I am talking about. When a crisis hits a family we all should want to get out of it as fast as possible. When we are faced with personal setbacks and there is an immediate way out of the setback, we should grab that option with both hands.

Yet, as we have noticed by now, that is seldom how life operates. It would honestly be awesome if it so happened that you get bankrupt today and tomorrow you are in the black. It would be perfect if I suffer a setback today and tomorrow I am totally out of it. That however is not what normally happens. *Generally, there is always a gap between the moment of a setback and the moment of a comeback.*

It is this gap that we need to address. Knowing what to do in that gap will determine how fast we can get our comeback, how much we can learn from the setback, and generally how well we will get to know who we are and what we really desire in life.

> *"The Law of Process is to birth the sensation of anticipation and hope"*
> —Dr. Mike Murdock

## Fear: The Enforcer of Setbacks

Another reason as to why people normally think that they have no options while in a difficult situation is plain old fear. You need to understand that the options available to us in a stuck state are seldom options that we are already familiar or comfortable with. Some of these options will work directly against our self esteem. Fear steps in when we are afraid of losing our status in society by accepting to take certain options that were not conventional before, or were up to that moment ascribed to people of a lesser class. A simple example is Ben's blatant refusal to find a cheaper house in a different locality so that he could manage paying his housing bills. He thought that if that is done, he would not be moving from glory to glory…that he would be accepting defeat and that he would be exiting the beloved middle class.

This alone has caused very many people their very sanity. It comes with the illusion that going a class lower is a permanent move. People do not want to be identified with 'going down'. However, if we only knew that at the moment, 'going down' is the preparation of a major high, we would not be afraid of that state anymore. We would take the cheaper house gladly as we mentally prepare for a comeback. With less pain and loads of bills to pay, our minds are now free to embark on the options available for a mighty come-back.

Fear also can plague people and incapacitate them. A stuck individual might be so afraid to even sit down and generate some options. Paradoxically, the antidote to fear is what fear makes us avoid doing—taking well needed action of any sort! So you would find someone saying that they have no options to work with…but the real story behind it all is that they are thoroughly afraid to think. Accepting the adversity is one of the best things we can do in order to get out of it. A scared individual might want to resort to faith. As much as faith is critical, it does not negate the stark reality of the present moment. In fact, faith finds its fulcrum in today's hardship to orchestrate the desired better outcome. In the end, that faith will still need to be activated by action. It is true that the opposite of faith is fear!

**Fire-fighting: Blinding people from seeing options**
Finally, one of the biggest reasons as to why we seldom provide ourselves with options is that we get bogged down with fighting fires adversity has brought. We tend to be more tactical than strategic. We tend to focus all our energies on keeping our heads above the water. We are encumbered with the load of putting food on the table and clothes on our back. We are so bogged down with protecting the little that we have, not wanting it to be taken away from us. All our energies are spent on clutching so tightly to the tangibles around us—the car, the house, the savings, and any other thing that we consider an asset. Our focus is mostly on not going down so much that we do not know how greatly we are emphasizing the 'down' the more we resort to this option.

> *"Success is how high you bounce when you hit the bottom"*
> —David Packard

Honestly, the options we can use while we are still obscure are seldom found on the surface. We might need to be deliberate in finding options. Naturally, the options on the surface include doing nothing, waiting, hoping, and protecting all we have at the moment. As you can see, all these options are simply reinforcing the stuck. Even if any of these options do work, eventually we will find ourselves back in the stuck state. These are not empowering options, but rather disempowering.

**Generating Options**
As already indicated, moments of adversity are largely influenced by our mental disposition. When we tell ourselves that we have no options, then we get stuck. Getting out of the adversity however is never necessarily a result of focusing on the tangibles…it is achieved by focusing on that which is intangible.

Let us take some time and examine Ben's life once again. We know that he is currently stuck yet doing nothing about it because he reckons that he has no options. Ben thinks that without money and a steady job, there is nothing he can do. He is so afraid of doing what the majority do—seek for a job because he reckons that without a degree, he has no chance.

As you can see, that inventory is just a quarter of an analysis that Ben could do. At any one point in time, we as human beings have the following:

- Strengths,
- Weaknesses,
- Opportunities,
- Threats.

For some reason, most people including Ben do take an inventory of their weaknesses, amplifying it so greatly that it blinds their strengths and opportunities. When it stays this way, eventually the *threats* even though not documented will certainly become a reality. Our threats are just that; threats. Yet if we do not notice those 'wake up calls' early, these threats give birth to more weaknesses.

Ben had so much going for himself.

1. He had already developed a 14 day coaching program…and had already acquired some clients before he lost his job. Some of these clients referred others and so on. In other words, this was on option worth leaning on. Did he pursue it? Nope. Why? The job loss made him feel inferior. Did the people he coached benefit? They did. Some even had their friends with children who had problems referred to Ben. Yet Ben was did not believe in himself to totally rely on the Coaching Practice to feed his family and pay his bills. But was this an option? You bet it was!

2. When Ben started jogging, he envisioned a documentary that he called, "My Jog To Success". The idea here was to create a documentary that would

inspire people to champion their own success from what they had in their hands…and in this case, the only option Ben had was jogging. Great concept at face value. Did he write it down? Yes. Did he develop it further? No. Did he seek funding? No. Could he have found someone who would have helped him do the scripting and the filming? Most probably. Did he look for that person? No. Why? He assumed that the process would take loads of cash which he did not have at that moment…so he did nothing.

3. Ben had actually been interviewed on Radio and TV stations. He could have taken the recordings of those interviews and included them on his social media thus enhance his brand. Did he do that? No. Why? That option did not have immediate monetary value…or so he thought.

4. Ben was a prolific writer. As a coach, he had realized that most of his coaching clients always complained that they wished someone would have taught them the success principles earlier. He devised a scheme to write a book aimed at encouraging parents to coach their kids in success principles as early as possible. He had all the time in the world to write the book since he was not in active employment. Did he write the book? Yes. Did he publish it? Nope. Why? He had no money to. Did he ask around for someone to fund the project? No. Why? He was afraid that people would say no. What did he do? He put the manuscript in the back burner. Could that book have been published? Yes. Could he have sold several copies? Probably. Could he have created himself a platform on Children Mentorship? Yes. Has he? No. Why? Money.

5. Ben actually got to do volunteer work with a Christian radio station as the 5:00 O'clock prayer general. His coach asked him to find a way to generate income from his listeners. Was that an option? Yes. The church policy however was not to raise money in exchange for prayers. Was this an option still? Yes. Attached are the testimonials of some of the listeners that interacted with Ben on his radio program. Did this have the capacity to give him cash immediately? Probably. How about a platform? Most definitely! Did he leverage this wonderful opportunity? Yes. He gave his very best. There are days he never had bus fare back home after ministering in at the station…but he went still. He gave his very best. That was a seed that was sowed. Ben actually did what he could do in his season of adversity. His wife and child could at times go hungry…but that did not stop Ben from doing this. It actually meant so much to Ben that to date, he still dreams about the impact that he created in service to his audience. Kudos to Ben for exploiting this option to the very end. One day, a listener texted in and thanked Ben for the wonderful job he was doing. She told Ben that he was free to ask anything he wanted. He did not heed that call immediately, until

two weeks later when he was stuck after ministering. He called her up for help. It turns out that she gave Ben a very big boost of financial assistance that helped him relocate his family from a mosquito infested house in a muddy village to a better housing unit, just before he was recalled by his former boss to go lead the organization in a different country!

6. He was married: Ben had married a beautiful girl who was his perfect compliment. She was filled with so much wisdom. She was a master dreamer and a songstress. I am not talking about just any songstress, I am talking about the who-is-who in the gospel music industry in the country Ben was living. Her music played in the popular mainstream Christian stations as well as secular stations. She had recorded more than 6 songs, three of which were crowd favorites. Couldn't Ben and his wife create an album of her music and sell? Of course they could. But they didn't because they sought perfection which never came.

These are just but few options that Ben would seek to explore while he still waited for his break. Unfortunately, the most he did was wait, and the least he did was to work with these options. As you can see, there are several reasons why Ben thought not to activate his options. Yet we know one thing: the options were available!

In the days of a setback, you might not need very many options to work with. You might just need one or two at a time. *Your comeback is more pronounced when you work with available options than when you wait for the situation to change.*

# CHAPTER 8:

# The Biggest Secret in God's Creation: Where are you Now?

*"I believe there are overriding principles that we should follow and be led by. That life is about constant, predictable patterns of change. And that as we approach the future; for all of us, the only constant factor will be our feelings and attitudes toward life".*

—Jim Rohn

Do you know one of the greatest secrets in how God structured life? That God is an Infinite Master of creation is as obvious as the sun that rises daily. Science has tried for years to understand how things in life work, their structures, their makeup and all. In fact, science has always tried to replicate creation itself, something that some people in other quarters of non-religion would really cherish so as to affirm that there is no God.

> *"If we are careful enough, we will realize that the cycles of success and hardship are directly proportional. One complements the other".*

The secret of Creation (and I know that there are many) is what these scientists need to work with, if they really have to replicate what God made…and if they can do that without any raw materials from God, that would be the day that God will be replaced, and that day is not coming any day soon, or ever.

We know that in life, everything is composed of parts. When you see my upper body in a car down the streets, you will not say, "I saw Lawrence's head in a car down the street", you will say, "I saw Lawrence in a car down the street". I am made of parts. Each part has components. When you separate the parts and the components, balance is lost and the equilibrium in life is distorted.

So behind the masterful art of creation God made, there are some secrets that hold the whole picture together. One of those secrets is this: God made things to operate in cycles and circles. God also made things to obey systems and processes. The moment we are ignorant of either cycles and circles and systems and processes, we get destabilized. The moment your try to make life happen in total disregard of systems, processes, cycles and circles, you are operating against nature and are bound to reap adversity.

Our studies in Biology tell us of the wonder of metamorphosis. Personally, I think most of us revel in the wonder of the butterfly and shriek at the sight of a caterpillar. Yet the caterpillar is an important part of the whole cycle of a butterfly.

Another wonder of nature that intrigues us all is the wild beast immigration. This happens almost to a pin point timing of a mathematical constant every year. It is triggered by the changes in nature that God created.

In terms of weather, we have summer, spring, winter and autumn. It is a perfect cycle that was set to repeat itself year in and year out, marking different seasons in the weather.

> *"Personally, I think most of us revel in the wonder of the butterfly and shriek at the sight of a caterpillar. Yet the caterpillar is an important part of the whole cycle of a butterfly".*

The formation of rain is an interesting cycle to study too, and so is the relationship between animals and plants in terms of sharing oxygen and carbon dioxide. Life is a masterpiece, only a fool would say that it randomly happened and there is no God behind it!

In our physical growth, we have stages. They might not run in a complete circle with one person, but immediately that one person gives birth to a son or a daughter, the cycle begins yet again.

**Let me say this again, one of the grandest secrets of creation is life operating in cycles! There is nothing living, whether made by man or created by God that does not obey this small secret.**

Knowing this secret can offer us great insights in setting ourselves up for our own comebacks after a setback. Not knowing this secret will be greatly detrimental to us in terms of building a strong resilience index during a life crisis.

If we are to talk about success, we have to realize that it has its cycle as well. If we are to talk about hardship, we need to know that it has its cycle. In fact, if we are careful enough, we will realize that the cycles of success and hardship are directly proportional. One complements the other.

One thing about a cycle is that it endures forever. The purpose of a cycle is to replenish and produce stronger and better lives as each cycle is repeated. Therefore, understanding the cycle of a typical life crisis is of absolute importance if we are to orchestrate major comebacks from each setback we will face in life.

No matter the color, creed, status or religious orientation, every human being faces some level of adversity at one point in their lives. In fact, if we were careful enough, we will realize that our lives are structured into one major cycle that revolves around crises and how we handle them.

Anthony Robbins says that there are two major motivators in people's lives: Pain and Pleasure. I could not agree more. In fact this cycle encompasses these two aspects of our lives in two formats: we are either in pursuit of pleasure or we are in a flight from pain. Take a look at your own life right now. Is this the truth? I bet it is.

The diagram below illustrates the cycle of crisis for all human beings:

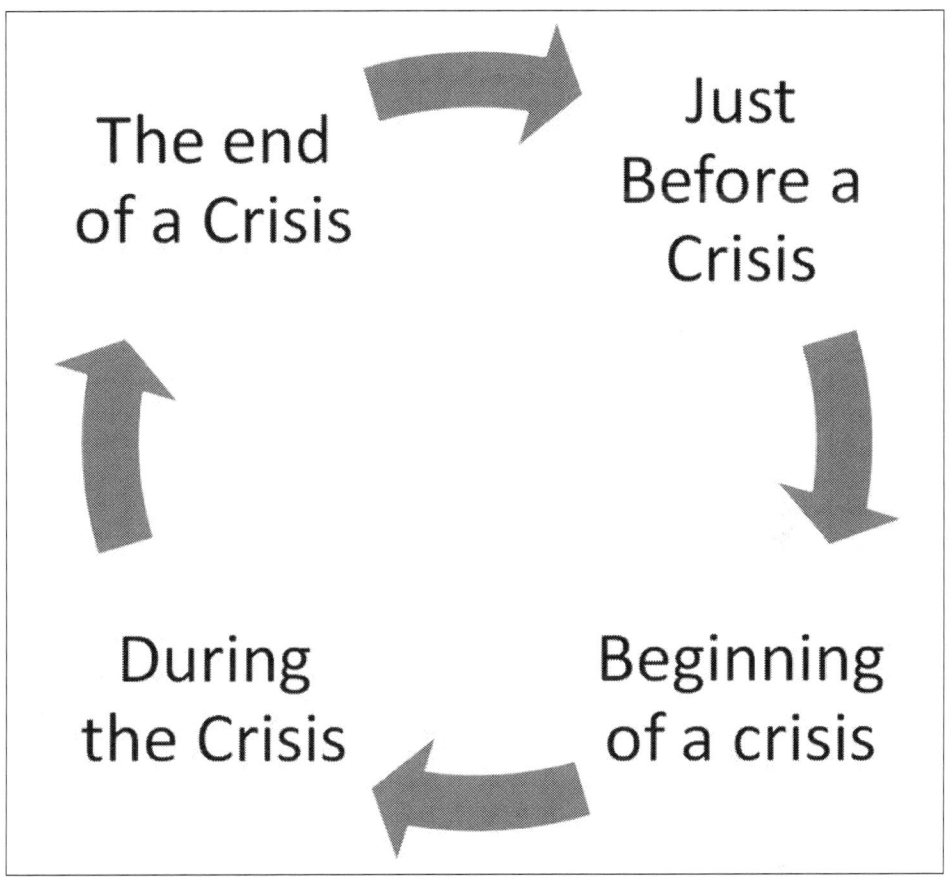

In reality, it may not be possible for anybody to live on earth without going through this cycle. Now, let us realize that I am not championing negatives here. All I am saying is that we are living in a fallen black world. The days of our lives will not be filled with pleasure from the first day to the last. We have to realize that we will experience setbacks, suffer heart breaks and generally get *feedback* we do not like.

Even the spiritually mature are never exempt from the cycle above. Now, the word crisis as used in the diagram can be interchanged by several other words just to bring my message into context. Words such as setback, failure, hardship, stuck and predicament can easily replace that strong word 'crisis' as used in the diagram.

Knowing what we know about setbacks, that they are paramount but not permanent to any life, the thing that matters most to us is to know how best to

> *"I think one of the most important things about our resilience index is to recognize whether the crisis is inevitable or not. That way, we get to navigate those murky waters better and at a higher resilience. There are some hardships that will inevitably go into the next phase of the cycle. There are also others that can be minimized and nipped in the bud before they can coalesce into bigger trouble"*

navigate the ship of our life in the days of turbulence. Very many people have come out better from a life crisis than before they encountered it. It is my assignment to show you exactly how you can be one of them.

**THE CYCLE EXPLAINED:**

### Phase 1-Just Before A Crisis: Take Heed

*"You may encounter many defeats, but you must not be defeated. In fact, it may be necessary to encounter the defeats, so you can know who you are, what you can rise from, how you can still come out of it."*
— Maya Angelou

On 21st September 2013, a gang of terrorists stormed into Westgate Mall, an up-market shopping outlet in Nairobi Kenya, shooting indiscriminately and hurling grenades at shoppers. After killing tens of them, they proceeded to stage a hostage crisis that lasted 3 days and was broadcast in all major news channels of the world as the main breaking news item.

At the end of that crisis, the Kenyan President announced that Kenya had ashamed its enemies and that the Kenyan Defense Forces (KDF) had prevailed. The number of people killed was 61, including prominent foreign nationals. At the time of writing, there are still many questions that are unanswered.

One thing that stood out, however, is that many Kenyan elected leaders as well as leading opinion leaders asked the President to send the chief of National Security Intelligence home without a medal. They asked that the President should not be soft in overhauling the entire department of intelligence in the country. According to them, there must have been some warning signs that went unheeded.

Well, I am not an intelligence expert or a security guru, yet I tend to agree with what these leaders are saying. What we must know however, is that God in his infinite wisdom has built within us a subtle system of intelligence that automatically sends us warning signs whenever things would go wrong. Normally this intelligence system works in Phase One of the Crisis cycle without fail.

Red flags, hunches. Butterflies in the stomach. Fear. Apprehension, and sometimes Dreams. If it is a relationship, you might notice the inconsistencies of your partner. She told you she was 23; you found out that it's actually a transposition error: she's actually 32. The investment company told you that you will get your dividends first week of next month, it's the third week and they have not communicated.

> *"God in his infinite wisdom has built within us a subtle system of intelligence that automatically sends us warning signs whenever things would go wrong"*

Everyone goes through this stage, and that is why emotional intelligence is critical. When people tend to make decisions based purely on emotions, they tend to accelerate the crisis. In fact, at this level, it is very easy to resort to 'the illusion of hope'. You start making excuses or rather give room for the inconsistencies. What you would not allow, you now do. You say, "It's OK, age is just a number". Well, if age was just a number, you would not be feeling uncomfortable about it, would you? Hoping against the warning systems (that uncomfortable feeling, that apprehension, fears and so on) would easily launch you into the next phase of the crisis cycle.

> *"You can't get rid of January simply by tearing it off the calendar. But here is what you can do: you can get stronger; you can get wiser; and you can get better".*
> —Jim Rohn

I think one of the most important things about our resilience index is to recognize whether the crisis is inevitable or not. That way, we get to navigate those murky waters better and at a higher resilience. There are some hardships that will inevitably go into the next phase of the cycle. There are also others that can be minimized and nipped in the bud before they can coalesce into bigger trouble. And even when that happens, your life will not necessarily go back to 'normal' as you once knew it. Even at this early stage of the cycle, there is a lot you can learn even if the crisis does not go all the way to the last phases.

For example, when Ben's company lost their first contract that was a major red flag for Ben to navigate the waters of his ultimate fear. That red flag would no doubt coalesce into the next phase of the crisis. Immediate action would have bought Ben some level of resilience in the years that followed. Waiting on it as Ben did would make it tougher to navigate out.

Just before the crisis, it is important to know that we cannot ignore the red flags at any cost. We need to be more objective than emotional, as early as possible. We also need to make sure that we take appropriate action to either nip the crisis in the bud, or get prepared to wade the murky waters ahead. To be forewarned is to be forearmed.

**WHAT TO DO JUST BEFORE A CRISIS.**

**Evaluate Immediately:** There is a big reason as to why those warning signs are being fired at you. The worst you can do right now is to ignore them. The best you can do is to immediately evaluate the nature of these warning signs and the capacity they pose to usher in a setback. Do you know how the Titanic sank? They ignored warning signals. How do you evaluate? You use a series of questions. You get your bias out of the picture and face the hard facts head on.

**Categorize the warning signs:** You need to know whether these warning signs are fired so you can adjust your direction or so you can get ready for the inevitable. This is absolutely critical. Again if we look at the example of the Titanic, research has shown that actually the ship was unsinkable only if it did not hit an iceberg. There was an audacious remark that 'even God would not sink the Titanic'. If the Titanic had changed course and avoided the iceberg, they might have survived. The Titanic crisis was not necessarily an inevitable one. Categorizing the warning will help you know exactly what action you need to take.

> "The secret in this level is to realize fast enough that things will never be the same again. Quick on its heels, we also need to realize that this change is only temporary. To be honest, very many people spend lots of time seeking to maintain the status quo. The longer you take trying to maintain your 'class' as the crisis begins, the longer it takes for you to get out of the crisis".

**Be as Objective as possible:** That you could face a crisis should be a possibility that you are willing to agree with. Your emotions should not shield you in the present comfort zone. It will only last a while if you choose to heed to your emotional voices. You need to be as objective as possible, which means you need to evaluate this warning signs from a neutral stand point. Most importantly, find out if your reasons for not heeding the warning are directly connected to protecting your comfort zone. That is how you would know whether you are being objective or not.

**Talk to Someone:** Do not under-estimate the power of a conversation. In one conversation, illusions that you might have over something can be tremendously altered! You should be having a personal confidant, a mentor, a coach, a spouse or someone you trust that you can talk to. People outside of the equation tend to be more objective. Look for people who care about your well being, and not those you are in direct competition with.

**Document Your Action Point:** You need to have a clear documentation of the nature of the warning signs and what you intend to do about them. Visit this website and download the Pre-Crisis Action Point template that will help you identify what exactly you need to do: http://life-signatures.com

> *"A smooth sea never made a skillful mariner"*
> —English Proverb

## Phase 2-The Beginning of The Crisis: Make Quick Adjustments

> *"What the caterpillar calls the end of the world, the master calls a butterfly"*
> —Richard Bach

What you feared is finally here. There is no more waiting. If it is losing the job, it has already happened. If it is losing your investments, it has already happened. If it is a career setback or a financial setback, by now you already are in it. You got here either because it was inevitable (outside your control) or you did not heed the warning signals that were sent earlier. You cannot waste time with 'a commission of enquiry on how this happened'. Now that you are here, what can you do to get out?

At this level, the quicker we adapt to the changes that are taking place, the much better. Dr. Mike Murdock says, *"The reason as to why the dinosaurs are extinct and cockroaches are still here is adaptation"*.

Adaptation does not mean you are giving up your dreams and pursuits. It only means you are accepting the changes in the environment and that despite these changes you remain focused on your life purpose. Sometimes, we lose lots of time fighting a crisis rather than learning it in order to navigate through it. At the beginning of the crisis, we need to realize that things will never be the same again. Most people at this level normally tend to clutch on things so tightly not wanting to let go.

People need change management skills at this level. The secret in this level is to realize fast enough that things will never be the same again. Quick on its heels, we also need to realize that this change is only temporary. Too many people spend lots of time seeking to maintain the status quo. The longer you take trying to maintain your 'class' as the crisis begins, the longer it takes for you to get out of the crisis.

Your emotional health is critical here, and it's likely to take a serious beating initially. This is compounded with the fight to maintain things at 'normal'.

We have to realize that there is great emotional strength gained when we accept early on that things will not be the same again, make the adjustments and move on. With this knowledge we are better placed to navigate our hardships.

This stage is so subtle in the way it merges with the next. For some people, this stage takes longer than others. The more you fight the crisis or stay in denial, the longer it takes. Your goal is to move through this stage as fast as possible. In reality, it is only you who can determine how long you can stay here. The secret is simple, yet not easy: Accept that things will never be the same again, but also acknowledge that the crisis is only temporary.

What to do at the beginning of a crisis:

**Make Psychological Adjustments:** Make no mistake about it. This phase is not as easy as it sounds, neither is it easy to make the necessary adjustments. It will be painful and difficult. The biggest adjustment you can make however is psychological. By accepting the reality of the crisis, you do make a major psychological adjustment that will help you through.

**Make 'Class' Adjustments:** I think the worst you can do in this phase is to continue insisting on living a lifestyle that you led just before the crisis hit. This is self defeatist. You need to immediately make the correct financial and lifestyle adjustments at the very beginning of the setback. You cannot continue eating sausages for breakfast when you just lost your job and have no steady income. You cannot insist on renting that expensive apartment while the crisis lasts.

You need to realize that making the adjustments is not permanent. It is obeying the changes that have taken place and shifting your options considerably.

**Review/Expand Your Action Points:** Change is the key word in this phase. You cannot continue to operate like you were in your 'normal' days. Things have changed and so your actions should. You need to document your daily action points that will govern your life as the setback lasts. This adjustment is in a bid to align yourself with the season and keep you productive. In the previous phase, you generated some action points from the download in the website. It is now time to review and expand this list. This is one of the most critical things to do; you will learn to love the list.

**Make Yourself a Promise of A Comeback:** I have talked so much about accepting early the arrival of the crisis. In order to keep our heads up, we need make ourselves a firm verbal promise that we will come out better. This is a simple affirmation that you can tell yourself over and over again every single day. When this is done, you are communicating to your subconscious mind about the possibilities that are there in the wake of the setback. When a setback comes, certainly your subconscious mind is laden with negative connotations about your demise. These are the illusions I talked about earlier. You get rid of these negative illusions through this process of affirmations.

**Talk to Someone:** When facing a tragedy, we tend to hide from people. That is one extreme. Another extreme is seek as many people as possible to get sympathy from them. One thing is for sure: when you seek the audience of a trusted friend, mentor, coach or spiritual leader, they are bound to give you much needed advice. I would prefer that you talk to a specialized coach because they tend to be very objective as they are professional. You will find out that talking helps a big lot. I think one of the worst things you can don at the beginning of a crisis is to suffer in silence. Talking to people who care will generate much needed hope as well as give you valuable pointers to use in orchestrating your comeback.

> *"No one who accomplished things would expect to avoid mistakes. Only those who do nothing make mistakes".*
> —Harry Truman

## Phase 3-During The Crisis: Choose to Learn

> *This thing that we call "failure" is not the falling down, but the staying down.*
> -Mary Pickford

One day after Ben's crisis had taken a major toll on him, he wrote his Coach the following:

"There is this great visionary I once knew. He had a lot going on for him. His future was bright. He had set his sights high and there was no stopping him.

He had and still does have so great potential. Something happened to him and he stopped dreaming. He spends most of his time in the house watching TV, and he seldom reads.
He has been waiting on a dream…nay, he has been waiting on several dreams that are now seemingly dead. Most of these dreams were detours from his vision. He thought that he could use the fruits accorded with these dreams to fuel his vision. So he stopped working on the vision, and embarked on waiting for the dreams.

The dreams are no more…and now he's back to nothing but the vision.

You know him, you have spoken to him again and again. He has been below your radar for months now, ostensibly waiting for the dreams to happen.

His name is Ben.

I am writing this to seek your help to get back on track. I hope we can converse at your convenience.

Blessings."

In this phase, you are well into the crisis. Most probably, the end of it is nowhere within sight. Obviously, things have changed *seemingly* for the worst. You do not want to be here but you are anyway.

For most people, their main pre-occupation is how to get out of the crisis. They are always looking for the end of the crisis. Some people postpone living altogether and resort to waiting until the crisis is gone. The normal that they used to know is not here and they want it badly.

This phase can be one of the most valuable phases of your life. I am not saying that this will be a comfortable phase. I am saying that what you can get out of this phase would be invaluable. You will not want to get back to this phase again, but most certainly, you will attribute your biggest life lessons to this season.

Your attitude is the greatest asset here. Since setbacks have lessons to teach us, we can either choose to learn these lessons or we can be forced to learn them. Either way, we will still learn.

A story is told of a certain Chinese waitress who served in a popular restaurant frequented mostly by English speaking people. Unfortunately for her, she did not speak English. That however did not deter her from offering exemplary service to the patrons of her restaurant. A certain couple tells of how so well they were served despite the fact that they were not able to communicate with the waitress. Her eyes were on them with total commitment, absolute concentration and anticipation. If anything went wrong, the waitress was already there to assist. If the couple showed any form of discomfort, she was there immediately to help. The couple felt that the waitress' eyes were on them at all times. Needless to say, they were blown away with the exemplary service.

The important thing about Stage 3 is the attitude we have as the crisis endures. We need to adopt the attitude of the Chinese waitress towards the crisis, milking out all the lessons that we can learn with top notch attentiveness. Remember that the reason life offers us this crisis is so that we can learn. We also need to realize that we normally repeat the same class in life until we learn the lesson that the class is offering.

This is what this book is all about. What do you do while in a crisis? Contrary to popular belief, there are very many options that you can generate that will help you navigate a crisis. This stage is the most important stage of the cycle. It is here that you choose to learn some things that you would have otherwise not learnt anywhere else. The most important thing during this stage is not to check out on life, but to re-invent yourself as the hardship lasts. It is prudent not to postpone living but to continuously look at the silver lining in the dark cloud. For the record, this stage is not fun at all. How you navigate out of it is largely dependent on how you handled the first two stages. Whereas in normal situations, you might wait for inspiration to come in order to do something, you will increasingly realize that you will have to motivate yourself to take action.

Your emotions are not your friends. They easily can lead to illusions as discussed earlier. Your greatest weapon at this stage is objectivity and consistent actions of resilience. What do you do while waiting for the crisis to pass? The answer to that crucial question could very well define how you will lead the rest of your life for the better.

## WHAT TO DO DURING THE CRISIS:

**Generate Action Points:** This is mostly what this book is written. During a crisis, many people seeing their previous lifestyle gone assume that the only thing that they can do is to get it back. So people do nothing or are stuck with just one option of getting their previous lifestyle back. In the next chapter, I will show you exactly how you can generate several options to use when stuck.

**Take Immediate Action:** Inactivity is the sweetest fodder for fear. Most probably you are sore afraid about your life during this crisis. In order to magnify that fear, the only thing you need to do is nothing. If you stop living and start waiting, you are making this phase to be one of the most difficult times in your life.

Taking action is important here. We saw that Ben's only available action during his crisis was to go out jogging. That action alone inspired him enough. He would come back with his mind racing about ideas that he could use. He thought about projects he could champion. He thought about documentaries he could make, and books he could write.

Ideas are the children of incessant action, and they are exactly what you need. Some ideas could be acted on immediately and some might need help to be actualized. Whatever the case, make sure you do something. The worst you can do at this phase is to wait while doing nothing.

**Track Your Progress:** When Ben started jogging, he noted several things. He noted how difficult it was at first. He then noted how it became more bearable. Then he decided to set a goal in terms of how much time he should take to finish his jogging routine. As he documented his progress, he became motivated not only to beat his personal best, but to also do better than that.

**Fight for Consistency:** Your action points need two things. Time and a place. In short, you need a timetable. Timetabling your actions enable you to hammer down a consistent routine. Your friend during a setback is not only to take action but to maintain a consistency that will in turn form character. This point alone would see you becoming a very resilient person at the end of the crisis.

**Document Your Lessons:** No doubt you will learn quite a lot. The reason for learning is to learn so you can be different. Some of the lessons you are learning in this season can be instrumental after the crisis is gone. Apart from documenting your lessons, you also need to document your ideas which will most definitely come as you take action during this phase. Prepare yourself to be a consultant, helping others who will be facing the same thing you are going through right now.

---

*Happiness is not the absence of problems, it is the ability to deal with them"*
—Steve Maraboli

---

## Phase 4-End of The Crisis: Build Reserves

Do you remember the first major crisis that Ben experienced in his life? I never really got to tell how Ben got out. He was fighting the crisis to no avail. He did not see himself retreating to the village. Even when he finally did get there, he never really put his feet down to learn anything. He was in constant denial, up until one day; he gathered courage to accept what had befallen him. He started participating in community life, in full abandon. From the moment he did this, it was only 60 days and a phone call summoned Ben back to the city, and he has never ever gone back to that level.

This does not say in any way that Ben became immune to tragedy. He in fact faced worse tragedies than this, but the point is that he never did go back to the same level. Your just ended tragedy should be a platform that you use to get to the next level of your life. How you handled level 3 will determine this. If you were mostly focused on escaping the tragedy and not learning the lessons, chances are that you will be back to this level later on, one way or another.

At the end of the crisis, you need to come up with a system that shows how you will live your life better, how you will help others with the lessons you have learnt.

This stage in the cycle is absolutely critical, yet it is one of the most unattended. Most people think that 'life has now come back to normal', so they continue life as 'normal'. In reality, your life after a crisis is never normal. It has changed, and you do need to change. Even the people who were using the strategy of hope alone are affected in this stage. The fasting diminishes, the prayers become shorter and routine rather than heartfelt and desperate. The spiritual exercises that were an absolute must are now replaced by other sizzling activities of the 'normal' life.

Lessons that were learnt in the crisis are easily forgotten. Life goes back to normal. What you used to do just before the crisis is the same thing you are doing now. For the record, life never went back to normal. Life changed. This level is about you taking a serious review about what you have just gone through.

- Could it have been prevented?
- Did you bring this to yourself?
- Did you act in the best possible way as the crisis lasted?
- Have you been affected mentally?
- Is your self esteem affected?
- Knowing what you now know,

> *"This stage in the cycle is absolutely critical, yet it is one of the most unattended. Most people think that 'life has now come back to normal', so they continue life as 'normal'. To be honest, your life after a crisis is never normal. It has changed, and you do need to change".*

what would you do differently?

The most important part of this stage however is how best you will build reserves with the knowledge you have to help you in the next level of this cycle…which will faithfully come as sure as the sun is out there every day.

Do you know the greatest reserve of all time? Most people focus their building of reserves wrongly. You are not building reserves primarily to maintain comfort. You are building reserves so that when a crisis or a setback comes, you will have time enough to handle your pressing needs as you make adjustments for a comeback before they run out!

No matter what level you ascend to in life, you will always have pressing needs. All of us do have them; they just vary from one person to another.

- What reserves are you building in your finances?
- What reserves are you building in your relationships?
- What reserves are you building in your health?
- What reserves are you building in your mental sphere?
- What reserves are you building in your businesses?

It is these reserves that will enable you to build a good resilience index, ready for the next crisis in your life. The absolute reason for hardships is to help us build reserves once we have gone through. Building these reserves happens when we are intentional about it, especially having learnt the lessons we have learnt from the hardship. It would be an absolute waste if by the time another life crisis comes by; we have little or no resilience.

Instead of thinking that life is normal, let's use the philosophy of the ant. This is the most 'normal' life you will experience, yet in a very short while, things will change:

**Ants think winter all summer:** Of course summer will not last forever. Winter is coming. What are we doing in preparation for winter? Summer is the best time to prepare for winter. You do not prepare for winter during winter. You prepare for it when in a good frame of mind, when healthy and strong. This happens best at stage 4 of the typical life crisis cycle. The ants will also gather all that they possibly can during the summer. In other words, there is no stop sign of gathering food (reserves) during the summer. This is exactly what we should be doing at stage four of the crisis.

**Ants think summer all winter:** We have already talked about this. Winter is temporary. It will go. You cannot give up hope and think that your entire life will be one long winter.

It is important for us to recognize what stage in the cycle we are at and act accordingly. That is one of the best bet in building a strong resilience index. Unfortunately, most people go through all the four stages of the cycle with the same attitude.

Interestingly enough, just as there are different phases in the cycle, there are also different people in life depending on the resilience index that they have or have not built.

## The anchor of the cycle

> *"Do all the good you can, by all the means you can, in all the ways you can, in all the places you can, at all the times you can, to all the people you can, as long as you ever can"*
> —John Wesley

Throughout this book, emphasis has been made on 'Life Purpose'. From the beginning of Ben's epic journey through life we have seen how this theme is the main anchor of the Life Crisis Cycle.

Regardless of what you face in your life, there will always be something either directly or remotely connected to your purpose in life. As life can only be understood going backwards, you will notice that at some point in time, what seemed to be 'dead years' to you actually did offer valuable input as far as your purpose is concerned.

At the end of each phase of the cycle, you need to take some time and re-evaluate your life as far as your life purpose is concerned. That would be instructive to do.

### Three Types of People in a Crisis: Which are you?

There are three levels of people in regard to how they handle a setback:

**Level Ones:**

They can as well never progress in the cycle. They graduate very first from before the crisis into the crisis and stay there! Why? Because they are mentally defeated and generally, they assume that they lack options. They see themselves being unable to do anything about the setback. They wait for an outside force to help them while at the same time negating anything and everything that they can hang on at the moment. When the wait and help does not come, they settle. They resign. They make negative adjustments. They accept the setback as permanent. Their spark of life purpose dwindles, fades and flickers at a far distance at a very long interval, sometimes prodded by another setback.

It is easy to tell who belongs to this group. They have a victim mentality. They describe themselves as the unfortunate. They recognize that they belong to a particular group in society that cannot lead. Their speech is full of complaints of the impossibilities of the now. Their talk is punctuated with the victories of the past. Their language shows that they long for a savior from someplace else. Their spirit is weak and they are scared of dreaming anything bigger than meeting their daily needs.

They can tell you exactly why they will not make it in life. They hang on to one excuse and use it to emasculate their powers. Such excuses include, "I do not have a degree", or even worse, "I do not have a man in the high places to help me".

The Level Ones will not have to think to enumerate to you all that they do not have. They have recited it again and again. Ben used to belong to this group. His biggest desire was to have a University Degree…and when he did not succeed in this one, it became his Achilles' heel.

Fear, ignorance, illiteracy and lack of inspiration are some of the things that keep the Level Ones from orchestrating their own comebacks. Contrary to popular belief, poverty is not a major catalyst to creating more Level Ones. It is the lack of knowledge.

Yet from this bunch have come great visionaries and world changers, movers and shakers of several spheres of life such as Business, Government, Religion and Philanthropy.

The story is told in Australia of a 26 year old illiterate man who had already resigned to fate that he would forever be a brick layer all his life. That of course changed when one day he heard a message of inspiration from the world changer Billy Graham in a crusade. He heard the message that all men were equal before the eyes of God.

At 26 years of age, Peter J. Daniels was not aspiring for anything other than be a champion boxer. He had been raised thinking that he was a bad boy, with a school teacher always telling him that he will never amount to anything. However, when information came, Peter J. Daniels started studying by himself, starting with a dictionary. He studied English as a language, psychology, history, economics and finance. He went into business and experienced setbacks of losing all his investments three times. However, Mr. Daniels turned all his setbacks, including that of being in Level One into major comebacks, becoming a multi-millionaire who would be appointed an Honorary Ambassador. In 2013 September, the following entry is made on Wikipedia about Peter J. Daniels

> Peter J. Daniels is an Australian life coach, writer, and professional speaker. Daniels has authored thirteen books, including How to Reach Your Life Goals and How to be Happy Though Rich. Daniels came from a disadvantaged background and was challenged with illiteracy in his early years. His family was third generation welfare recipients, he has two alcoholic brothers, 4 fathers and 2 mothers. Many of his relatives have been in jail. He failed at every grade in school and became a bricklayer. At 26 years of age he was hopelessly in debt, and attended a Billy Graham Crusade on 25 May 1959. He attributes his life change and subsequent success to that meeting.
>
> After reading 2,000 biographies, Daniels went into business three times, failing each time, but avoiding bankruptcy. He subsequently managed to build a large real estate business in Australia and South East Asia and serves as a director and chairman on a range of international boards.

## Level Twos:

They are slightly different from Level Ones in that they recognize that the crisis is temporary. However, like the level ones, they do not do anything about the setback they are facing. They feel so incapacitated and succumb to the illusion that there is nothing they can do to remedy the situation or at least to make the best out of it. Their biggest asset is time… paradoxically. They know that at one point in time, the current crisis will end. So they abdicate nearly everything to the passage of time.

Of course it is easy to recognize the Level Twos. These are the 'hopeful' people. Their speech is full of the phrase 'one day'. They cannot wait for the future to come…the problem is that they are doing nothing towards it today. Unlike the Level Ones, this group knows that at least they deserve a better life. Their greatest weapon therefore is their speech. They proclaim victory in the face of defeat. They also become so spiritually heightened in order to increase their chances of the better future. These are the majority who develop the strategy of hope as discussed in Chapter Four.

The Level Twos seldom learn a lesson from their setbacks. The only lessons they will learn are those forced on them by the crisis. At the end of the crisis they have developed this big fear for setbacks in life. When another setback comes their way, they will handle it the same way they did the previous: outwait it.

A vast majority of the human population fall in this category. They have recognized that life is not a straight line. They also do know that life being cumbersome; still they deserve some level of comfort. That is why they will remain defiant when a crisis beckons. They tend to hang on everything they know and everything they have, never wanting to let go.

Ben's story is a typical example of a Level Two.

### Level Threes:

It is my desire that everyone will be at this level at any time a crisis hits them. These are the resilient. They know that what does not kill them will make them better. They are pro-active. They understand the full process of a life crisis and know how best to leverage its lessons. Unlike the Level Twos who are forced to learn some lessons from the crisis, the Level Threes are consummate learners who are bent on milking to the dregs the rich nuggets of life that could never be bought by any resources on earth.

Like the Level Twos, they understand that the setback is just that: a setback. They understand that the crisis is temporary. The Level Threes are people who are driven. Before the crisis, they were working on being a blessing on earth. At the crisis, they still do that, albeit at a slower pace. They understand that the crisis is as useful to them as the pupa stage is in the cycle of a butterfly's metamorphosis. The Level Threes will consequently refine their vision, become deeper in their spirits and ultimately prepare themselves to be better when they come out.

> *"And once the storm is over, you won't remember how you made it through, how you managed to survive. You won't even be sure, whether the storm is really over. But one thing is certain. When you come out of the storm, you won't be the same person who walked in. That's what this storm's all about."*
> -Haruki Murakami

One major thing about the Level Threes is that to them, the present is as critical as the future. They identify each and every opportunity at the present. They tend to use the principle of 'what can I do now?' It has proverbially been said that "when life throws you a lemon, make a lemonade out of it". This is exactly what the Level Threes do. It has also been said that "Necessity is the mother of invention". This statement holds true to the Level Threes, that out of their ashes, they paint beauties.

We must note however that it is not just necessity that is causing the Level

Threes to make Lemonade out of Lemon; it is their dreams that fuel their resilience. One of their biggest distinguishing factors is that they have a clear sense of destiny. The setback therefore is an event to them. It is not the defining factor of their lives. Their sense of destiny is not snuffed out by the setback; it is rather brought to a place of refining and reflection. It is made clear as their hearts are prepared. Ben had this sense of destiny upon his life when he talked to Jackie his friend back at college.

The biggest advantage the Level Threes have over the previous levels is that they tend to navigate setbacks faster. It is like their days of adversity are shortened, which is the biggest desire of every human being at any level.

> "One major thing about the Level Threes is that to them, the present is as critical as the future. They identify each and every opportunity at the present. They tend to use the principle of 'what can I do now?'"

Level Threes are different from the other two levels in the following ways:

- Their Attitude
- Their Speech
- Their Proactivity
- Their capacity
- Their knowledge

We all need help when we encounter setbacks. I have prepared 21 strong points that you can use when you find yourself in a crisis in your life. Let me say this, strange as it may seem, I am not sure that these 21 points will work! Why would I give you nuggets that I am not sure will work?

There is a simple reason to this: All formulas have the other part that we never talk about. All formulas are not guaranteed to function. The other part of a secret or a formula or a method or a law or a principle is you. In other words, if you do not use the methods, if you do not apply the formula, if you do not practice what you have been taught, then there is no guarantee that you will succeed.

I can only guarantee your coming out of a setback a better and deeper you if you do your part. Chances are that you honestly want to do exactly that, and that is why a book like this is in your hands. That is why you have read well up to this chapter.

I must say that the 21 options I will share with you are a whole mixture. Some options are plain old obvious. Some are easy to implement, others are hard. Some are straight-forward, others are a bit cumbersome. The most important ingredient to these options is you: how well you understand them and how best you put them in practice.

The above nuggets are so critical for you to note. At the end of the day, it is those little foxes that spoil the vine. It is just a small amount of yeast that works up in the whole dough. It is important that you cushion yourself in your moment of crisis. When you find yourself in a hole, you do not dig deeper…you first of all stop digging, then you can figure the way out.

# CHAPTER 9:

# 21 Ways To Come Out Better: Nuggets to Navigate a Crisis

"Abundance is about focusing on what you have and what you can do, not on what you don't have and what you think you can't do"
–Kim George

As already discussed, when we hit a crisis, we normally tend to negate everything good that is happening for us. The crisis is magnified so greatly that we cannot see any positives. In fact we even do not take stock of anything positive that we have at all. Instead of doing a SWOT analysis of our lives, we mostly embark on doing a WT analysis - we focus on our Weaknesses and Threats, and seldom consider our Strengths and our Opportunities.

Our thinking is mostly external—we look for help from anywhere else apart from us. Whenever we think about ourselves, it normally is about the weaknesses we have and the threats we will be facing. Granted, it is only human to behave that way…yet if this continues over time it affirms our crisis and makes it even more uncomfortable. We will be unable to see any good that can come out of it. In fact we prolong the setback by this kind of thinking.

> *"Do what you can where you are with what you have"*
> ~ Quote

We need to know that that which we know at the moment – however simple it might be to us— can be exactly what we need for our comeback. Each of us is responsible for our own light that shines, and not for that which we have not discovered. The highest calling in life is to do something with whatever revelation we have acquired… or that which has been illuminated in our lives.

This revelation varies from person to person, region to region, race to race. Nobody lacks revelation. Each one has some form of illumination. The genesis of being stuck is wishing you had someone else's revelation while at the same time neglecting what you have right now.

Obviously, the first thing we need to do in order to orchestrate our comeback is to analyze the situation in order to generate as many options as possible. There are three places where you can look for valuable information to guide you out of the setback you have:

- Internally
- Intimately and Externally
- Infinitely

You have probably heard this quote:

> *"We are human beings…not human doings"*

As we take a look at the 21 options that I am offering for turning your setbacks into comebacks, it is important to realize that our state of being is perhaps the most important aspect of orchestrating our comebacks.

The options that I am discussing are not necessarily focusing on doing things. I honestly think that good results come from doings that stem from healthy being. Interestingly enough, being also stems from doing! The question is: which one comes first? Which one has the deeper priority? Obviously it is working on our mental state.

We have already said that many people do not work on their 'being' mostly because there is no direct or immediate monetary gain that comes from this strategy. As such, we are less motivated to work on our being but we get highly charged up to do something that will guarantee an immediate comeback from a crisis.

When we are comfortable with lack of action in the wake of many options, we are eroding our value. However, at times, it is important to be still, work on getting a deeper more meaningful state before a massive re-launch. This is what is normally called obscurity. What a massive season that life offers us—to be obscure to the world. It is a time to work on our 'being' with no interruptions from the media and from our fans. Mostly, this moment is served best at a time of a setback.

Consider the eagle. When an eagle grows old, his feathers become weak and cannot take him as fast as he would like. When he feels weak and about to die, he retires to a place far away in the rocks. While there, he plucks out every feather on his body until he is completely bare. He stays in this hiding place until he has grown new feathers, then he can come out brand new.

If you would work on your 'being', chances are that this setback you are facing today is a major blessing. It is a setup for your massive comeback. You will come out. Yet you will not just come out. You will come out better, deeper, wiser, sharper and new. Friend, this is the ultimate come-back from a setback.

## KNOWING WHAT YOU HAVE

### 1. Separate Illusion From Reality:
My definition of an illusion is simple: An illusion is a wrong and mostly negative interpretation of feedback only at face value. An illusion can be created in a split second with certain feedback, and if left to reign supreme, it can cause you to believe a lie. You need to realize that sometimes, the process of getting information, making a false interpretation and believing the interpretation can happen in less than a minute… basically, in split seconds! Herein lays

one of the greatest downfalls of many people when in a crisis… believing that something is worse than it really is, or ever could be.

The power of a belief cannot be over-emphasized. Beliefs are based on information or in our case, feedback. Any crisis in our life, any setback we experience is laden with lots of information. For the most part, the information that people act on is what I call 'surface information'. They form a belief based on what 'appears' rather than what really is. All our voluntary actions are linked to a belief, either directly or indirectly. The same applies when we do not take action. It is mostly because of a belief.

This belief can be over a period of time or even over a life-time. This false impression is normally created in the very first seconds of a crisis. For example, a Sales Manager might get feedback that shows dismal performance of his team's weekly sales. If the Manager does not critically analyze the situation, he may start operating under a general false impression that he will fail at the end of the year. He might go along with that reasoning that failure will cost him his job. When this happens, his self esteem is dealt a major blow which in turn influences the way he behaves on a daily basis. He starts seeing himself as a failure and on the list of those that would be done away with. Consequently, his actions will affirm what the illusion spells. Instead of going out more, he might shrink back. Instead of seeing his team as talented and able, he loses confidence in them altogether, which in turn affects their performance. In the end, the illusion becomes a self fulfilling prophecy.

It is true from the feedback that if that situation continued, it might actually result in what he fears—the loss of his job. Every time you are afraid of something, you need to check and find out if that fear is based on what is real, or on a false impression of what is real. There is no better story to illustrate this than the story we have shared of Nick Sitzman as told in the previous chapter.

One of the reasons as to why people tend to believe in illusions at first than to analyze setbacks is that they have an ultimate fear. A wife can be afraid that her husband could cheat on her. If she goes through the whole process in her thoughts as the Sales Manager we have discussed, chances really are that that could become a self fulfilling prophecy.

## 2. Identify, Document and Communicate Your Ultimate Fear
No doubt that the biggest thing that mostly runs out of our control during an adversity is our emotions. The emotion of fear alone can easily incapacitate a soul to paralysis. There are several things that can be done to gain emotional healing or mastery during a crisis. Talking to people can help you calm down.

Listening to people who faced the same thing and came out can also help. However, after gaining some stability over your emotions, it is important that you sit down and really identify your life's biggest fear.

It is important to document what we are really afraid of. Documenting your ultimate fear does not mean that you are ready to accept it, roll over and play dead. Most people do not want to do this because it is uncomfortable. They do not even want to mention it. They tend to think that identifying and documenting your fear goes against the tenets of positive thinking. To some level, positive thinking must move us from one point to a much better point.

It therefore pays a lot to know exactly what point we are desiring to move from. It is important to intimately come to terms with what our deepest fear is. There is plenty of relief and even healing that is orchestrated immediately we state what we are afraid of. The main reason for doing this is to help us to identify the options we can use to either:

- Assume or avoid the fear
- Put the fear in the correct perspective
- Reject the fear
- Face the fear
- Live with the fear through its temporary reign

Your fear might be the loss of your status in society. Let's extrapolate this for a minute. If you lose your status in society, it would mean that your self esteem will suffer. It would mean that you will not be accepted in certain social circles you previously operated in. It would mean that you would not be respected like you have been.

However, if you really thought it through, you would realize that your self esteem, respect from others, acceptance by others and ultimately your status in society might not come from what this setback is taking from you.

Let me explain using Ben's example. When the setback of the job loss came to Ben, he thought moving into a cheaper housing unit would negatively impact his status. His ultimate fear was perceived change of status. However, if you come to think about it, status is overrated. It does not come from the things we have, but from who we are.

A story is told that during those infamous yeas of slave trade, a certain batch of Africans got to the camp of one slave owner. He noticed that amongst this batch, there was a stubborn and belligerent young man who was openly disobedient especially when forced to squat, kneel or sit. When the slave trader asked about the boy, he got this reply from the handlers: "He is the son of a king back home, and he has not forgotten that!"

Identifying and documenting your fears is certainly a sure way of giving you the correct perspective about it. Writing about your ultimate fear can be done using the following format.

I feel so ... that (mention the type of the crisis, e.g. I have lost my job)

With this [mention the loss/setback e.g. job] (mention all the benefits that accrued before the setback)

I am afraid that I might no longer have these benefits for a some time

This makes me feel so scared of (mention your ultimate fear)

After doing this, it is easy to put that ultimate fear into perspective. You might have written that your ultimate fear is 'to be poor' for example. You now have the 'enemy' in sight and you can deal with this fear accordingly.

Communicating your ultimate fear is equally critical. It is important to talk about it vulnerably to someone trustworthy. The fear of your ultimate fear can easily paralyze you…but then again you might realize later on that the fear of your ultimate fear was not warranted. You might realize that it was an illusion all along.

Men have the male ego factor. So when a setback comes, they withdraw into their 'cave' and agonize over it. If he is married, this state causes a major black cloud to hover over the entire family. A husband should communicate to his wife and tell her exactly what he's afraid of…yet there is a balance. Wives must be worthy of being told such bad news. Women are a great source of comfort to men. But the man will only be at peace knowing he will not be judged, nagged, or have his ego trampled on. So women need to hear the man out and understand his fear. In fact, women need to affirm their men again and again. A man can do wonders when he knows that a certain special woman believes in him…but I digress.

Apart from close friends and relatives, we can talk to the following professional people about our fears:

- A Pastor
- A counselor
- A Life Coach
- A Mentor

Remember, do not be silent. Silence can kill. Keep talking.

## 3. Analyze your setback

"There are four ways to respond to crisis: Maximize it, Minimize it, Advertize it, Analyze it. Maximizing is to exaggerate the crisis. Minimizing is to understate the crisis. Advertising is to tell the whole world about it. Analyzing is extracting useful information from it" – Dr. Mike Murdock's Morning Motivation, September 2$^{nd}$ 2013.

In the previous chapter, we talked about making adjustments at the beginning of a crisis. This is important especially after we have analyzed the crisis deeply to extract enough information that we can work with immediately.

I have prepared a comprehensive paper that you can use to analyze your setback. This is available as a free download from http://life-sinatures.com.

A crisis really is about what you are losing control of. It is important to put this 'loss of control in the correct perspective. As much as there is a lot of focus on what you cannot control at the moment, we also need to realize that there are simple, yet powerful things that we are directly in control of. If your liberties, rights and freedom have not been taken away from you, then you are pretty much in control of the critical things.

It would be very prudent to sit down and do an analysis of what exactly you are in control of and what you are not. In doing this you are generating as many options as possible with the philosophy of doing what you can, where you are and with what you have!

For example, Sam Walton, the founder of Walmart was the world's richest at some point in time. In fact Wikipedia reports that Bill Gates only became the richest man in the world after the death of Sam Walton. Reading about Sam Walton's life, you will notice that at one point he worked odd jobs including waiting tables. He was doing what he could do at that moment in time. You can find his intriguing story by searching 'Sam Walton' on http://wikipedia.com

Just the fact that you have lost control over some things does not necessarily mean that you have lost control over your life. It should not therefore be that you are doing nothing because you lost control of part of your life. What you have in your hand right now, indeed what you are in charge of at the moment could very well be the key that will unlock major things in your life.

Analyzing what you are not in control of is important. It gives you an opportunity to figure out what you can do with what you are not in control of:

- You could decide to do nothing about it
- You could decide to seek help with it
- You could decide if that area of your life is really worth the trouble.

Analyzing your setback provides you with the needed information in the wake of the following options:

a) **Accepting and Imploding:** In a split second, you can choose to either live in denial or come to terms with what exactly is happening. Imploding means that you are collapsing in an inward explosion…accepting the setback, but you are bottling everything inside. It is a choice, but we know it is not a conscious one.

b) **Accepting and shrinking:** This happens when you are initially overwhelmed with not only the setback but also the impending repercussions of the setback. The more you find yourself isolated, the easier it is to shrink back from life.

c) **Accepting and blaming:** You could spend a considerable amount of time apportioning blame, digging up the cause and justifying why you are not responsible for the crisis you are in. "I am jobless because my parents did not take me to University, I would be having many job offers".

d) **Accepting, making it your personal responsibility to orchestrate a come-back:** This is obviously the better option. Yet taking personal responsibility for your comeback would come better if you document some action points and create a plan for your comeback.

## 4. Analyze your life

You need to take a whole weekend to analyze your life. This setback has provided you the grand opportunity to be extremely reflective. Most probably you have major lingering questions in your mind right now. You might be wondering the reason of your birth. You might even be thinking about the reason of your existence at the moment. You might be fantasizing how better it would be to be non-existent. I can tell you that you are alive for a reason, although going through pain at the moment. Your family needs you, your friends need you, and yes, the world needs you.

This is a major opportunity for you to really do a serious review and analysis of your life. You might not have had this chance before, but right now, this is the most perfect opportunity to reflect, review and analyze the critical aspects of your existence. History tends to repeat itself, which is why you need to look at your past and analyze it. Your childhood as well as your recent past can provide you with valuable information about your history.

Someone said that life is 10% what happens to us and 90% how we react to it. Personally, setbacks have been the greatest catalysts of my life revivals. As you do this analysis, it is important that you realize how you have either been on the driving seat of your life or otherwise. Did you have a direction that you were taking? You need to find out if your life has been one big cycle that many people go through religiously without having a clear knowledge about its meaning and purpose. Maybe this could be the cause of your crisis, and if you do not deal with it now, it is bound to happen again.

- What's your vision?
- What's your Life Mission?
- What's your life purpose?
- What are your values?
- How do you want to be remembered?

These have been recurring themes throughout this book, and I am sure that by now you have probably thought once or twice about the meaning of your life. It is critical.

Again, time and space do not allow me to document everything about your life analysis. You can find out how this is done from http://life-signatures.com

> *"Something you have is the seed for something you do not have"*
> –Dr. Mike Murdock

**5. Analyze Your Potential:**
This is one of the biggest blessings you can bequeath yourself. For some reason, we all know that we have potential to do things. Life might have worked negatively on us just like the crisis you could be in is trying to prove and so the tendency in a crisis is look down on our potential. The biggest casualty of setbacks in life is usually your personal potential. If a crisis is not handled well, your potential can easily get eroded with every setback that comes your way.

Therefore, an analysis of your potential is extremely important. You need to remind yourself of how great you can be if you really put yourself to it. I read the story of Sir Winston Churchill who found a newspaper article that talked positively about him. He cut it out and put it in his pocket, reading it occasionally to encourage himself.

The analysis you will do at this level of a crisis forms a bedrock and strong foundation of your legacy. This means that you can always do this analysis even when out of the crisis, and chances are that at that time, it might be greater than it was during the crisis.

Everyone, including a day-old baby, has potential. Unfortunately, very few people take time to analyze it. Again, your crisis or hardship is a major setup for you to dig deep into your 'acres of diamonds' and discover your full potential. One day while listening to Peter J. Daniels, I heard him talk about potential from a very different perspective. The following system is credited to him. It helps us in our analysis of our potential:

**The four questions—Peter J Daniels:**
- At what age have you set yourself to reach your full potential that God might maximize your life?
- Could you tell me in 50 pages or more, what your full potential is in every area of your life?
- Accepting your full potential at 100% what percentage rating would you give yourself right now?
- Accepting the deficiencies between the two scores, what plan are you putting in place to take up the shortfall and win?

I think it is time to write your first book—your 50 pages of your personal potential.

*"Hold yourself to a higher standard than anybody else expects of you, never excuse yourself"*
–Henry Ward Beecher

**6. Analyze your S.W.O.T:**
I think it is increasingly being illuminated in our day and age that every person is a corporation. The earlier we let this information sink in the better. I am the Chief Executive Officer of my life. I am the Chief Financial Officer, Chief Marketing Officer as well as the Sales Executive of my life. I his book, 'What's Your Genius?' Jay Niblic says that we are to adopt the title of Self Executive Officer (SEO).

Any corporation worth its salt would always make strategic plans either as a proactive measure (mostly) or in response of changes in either the internal or external environment. In these plans, the organization would detail to utmost clarity what its strengths, opportunities, weaknesses and threats are. This document is one of the most powerful documents that an organization can have. Each element of the SWOT has action points.

As you continue to look at the options that you have in the setback you are experiencing, your SWOT analysis gives you invaluable action points. The SWOT of course is done when you have a direction that you are taking. That is why the previous points are absolutely critical. If you have analyzed your life and known your potential, this is the very next step that you can take. Again, your setback is simply a setup for you to unearth your SWOT.

There is so much to talk about SWOT and how exactly you can be able to do it. At face value, you should be able to do your personal analysis in this area. People have literally had revivals in their lives when they did this exercise. We shared the story of Joe Vitale ˙ who at one time was broke and living in his car. Another person who had a massive revival is Anthony Robbins. When he did his SWOT, he realized that he was sabotaging himself in several areas. He also realized that he was the master of his own destiny. He has turned his life around massively and is in the process of helping millions others around the world do the same.

I must admit that a SWOT analysis is not an easy thing to do. Ben never liked hearing of his weaknesses. He was afraid to hear anything negative about his life. So when you are in a crisis, you just must as well face it and deal with it.

I should also tell you that a personal SWOT analysis could be the biggest wake-up call that you can give yourself. If you are thorough about this, chances are that after this crisis is over, you will tackle life with new zeal, a new purpose being fueled with the knowledge of what you possibly can do if you put your mind to it. The good news is that the crisis will end. The setback has its timeframe. It will go.

One final thing about the SWOT analysis is that you do not just do it for the sake of knowing. You do it with the desire to take decisive actions immediately, in the interim and in the long term.

I cannot get over this SWOT analysis. It is a rich thing to do. For more pointers on how you can do this, visit http://life-signatures.com

### 7. Define Your Personal Brand:
I believe this is one of the most resourceful activities you can do while in a crisis…analyzing your brand. We need to know that everyone has a personal brand. We just need three things with our brands: Knowing it, owning it and showing it. I think at the level of a crisis, if you do not know what your personal brand is yet, this is the perfect time to define it. A personal brand is simply the value that you are known to provide to your audience. It is what your audience or other people are talking about you. If you will not be intentional

about it, you will not be able to have it. The good thing about a personal brand is that you do not need loads of cash to know it, own it and show it.

We have seen that during a crisis, one of the biggest illusions that people have is that they do not have any options to work with. We have also seen that a major assumption that people make is that if what you are engaged in at the moment does not provide direct escape from the crisis or does not at least try to alleviate your hardship, then it is not worth it.

However, you will notice that a Personal Brand is what in the end (after the crisis) will guarantee you repeated income through provision of much needed value to your audience. What a better time to be obscure and work on your Personal Brand than this time.

Again, let me say this: it is the simple little things that matter. Working on your personal brand is a simple thing. It can actually take you less than a week to really clearly define what your brand is. I will show you exactly how this is done on my website: http://life-signatures.com

Your personal brand is one wealth of an option that you should work on during your crisis.

**8. Dream and Document your future:**
What a better time to stare at your crisis and defiantly dare to dream again! At this point in time, I have to tell you that you do not have to hold yourself responsible for the fruition of your dreams. Your job is to dream. I am not talking about wishing…I am talking about deeply desiring a much better and improved life.

Frankly, you deserve it. That is why you are alive. If you did not deserve a life of your dreams, you would be in the grave by now. But you are still here. A crisis tends to break your dreams. The antidote is to dream. Granted, you are facing some limitations at the moment. It is therefore possible that your dreams might be 'shy'. Do not worry. I assure you that with time, your dreams will evolve and become bigger.

Many people probably don't know rich Shelton. I heard him speak more than a decade ago. As a young man, his biggest dream was to be a garbage collector. This dream was influenced by what he saw and what environment he was in. He thought that those guys working on the garbage trucks really looked cool, and his greatest dream as a young man was to be one of them.

You probably know the author of several books including "Battlefield of the

Mind", "Me and my Big Mouth", as well as "Reduce me to love" among many others. Her name is Joyce Meyer, and she appears on television around the world daily with a reach of over 1 Million people across the globe.

Her dream was to hold a woman's bible study fellowship occasionally at her home. Do you know who her pastor was? You might not guess it…but he is the guy who wanted to be a garbage collector. Pastor Rick Shelton.

Dreaming should be paramount, regardless of what situation you find yourself in. I dare say that dreams can even be immortal. They never die even if you try to assassinate them.

Now, do not just dream. Take some time and document your dreams. This is what is popularly known as 'goal-setting'. In Despite the fact that most people know how to set goals, few actually do this. For more about this, check out this article titled: "To Wed or Not To Wed, That is the Question" from : http://life-signatures.com

I have also included a comprehensive goal-setting strategy that you can find online to help you in times of crisis.

> *"People can take everything from you but they cannot take away your dreams"*
> –Peter J Daniels

Remember what Ben's wife did? She set up a vision board filled with pictures of things she would like to have and places she would love to visit. In her vision board, there was a family car, Ben's car, a flight, a nice house with beautiful interiors and of course some dollars. You can paint your house for a better future with such like pictures. This is what tangible dreaming is all about.

I must admit that Goal-Setting is the single most explosive way of generating instant options especially while you are in a crisis. It should be a paramount thing we do during all the phases of the cycles of our lives.

### 9. Create Your Personal Definition of Success:
Success is continuous. This means that there will always be something you want to reach out for after attaining what you had already desired. There are millions of definitions for success. I think it is a great disservice to yourself if you did not know how personal success to you looks like. By the way, chances are that many people could be in a crisis because they took a wrong path to success following someone else's definition. Success is as personal as it can get. My joy could not necessarily be yours. One man's meat is another man's

poison.

Have you identified what success really means to you? Are the things you are pursuing at the moment in the name of success really worth the effort? If you are in a crisis because you took the correct path to pursuing your success, good! Your successful navigation out of the setback will provide you with the needed resilience. However, if you are experiencing a setback because you took the wrong path, it is time to change.

The clearer you get in defining what success means to you, the more you start appreciating the things that are going well for you. You need to realize that what people praise you for is not necessarily what success is. In fact, I have realized that many people are mostly critics. They only join bandwagons of praising the 'world class'. If you are waiting for someone to praise you, you might wait for long.

In the same breathe, if someone criticizes you or makes negative comments about something that you are doing, it does not mean that you stop doing it, neither does it mean that you have failed.

In its basic form, success is what matters to you, and not someone else. Today, you need to define what it is for you. You must surely remember the story of the rich man and the fisherman back in chapter 6. Although it was a simple story, it has a very powerful nugget of asking, "And then what?" until you finally define what success means to you.

Start by stating what success means to you in a simple line, e.g. "Success to me means having a million dollars in the bank". Follow this with asking yourself, "And then what?" or "What would this do for me?" Answer that question too. Repeat that process until you fully identify what success means to you.

Chances are that after you have done this, you might realize that you are already successful or you are on the path to it, and what you are facing is a temporary setback.

Once you have identified what success means to you, do not let anything shake that definition out of your mind. Start painting pictures about it. Keep visualizing it. Make a vision board about it. Keep it in your sight. Of course the most logical thing would be to ask yourself what you can do towards attaining it now. I am sure you will have options that are so simple and readily available.

**10. Take action:**

This is what this book is about, taking action even in a crisis. Andrew Rugasira is the CEO of a company called 'Good African Coffee'. If you searched for him on the Internet, you will find out that one of the things he popularly said was this: "No country has ever prospered through handouts". That is a very stern statement, seeing that Andrew is a Ugandan, a country in East Africa that has depended quite a bit on foreign aid to expand its economy.

It is most definitely a natural instinct to seek 'aid' when you deem yourself 'incapacitated' to make it on your own. Make no mistake about it, there is a firm place for assistance from 'outside' while you are in a crisis. This however does not mean that you have nothing that you can do.

By now, through the exercises that I have provided, you should have generated major action points. By now, you should be having a time-table that shows what you will do at what time.

---

*"What we think or what we know or what we believe is, in the end, of little consequence. The only consequence is what we do"*
–Quote

---

Nothing is more valuable to you at this time than you to be engaged in a worthy enterprise. I am not talking about a job. I am talking about taking inspired action on things that come from within you.

You grow from taking action, and seldom from waiting. You also grow from taking action more than you do from receiving 'aid'. Normally, your worth and your self esteem is eroded through inaction. However, your esteem and essence is normally built greatly when you take any form of positive action.

Do you want ideas? There is a place where you can get them. It is when you are actively involved in something. For Ben, it was jogging. From it, he thought he would do a documentary titled, "My Jog to Success". He thought he would write a book about it too. Probably you are reading the said book with a different title!

My point is, when a crisis hits, we tend to shrink back from life. We tend to think that we will just 'out-wait' the crisis. Well, as we have already seen, there are several things that can make your hands full while you are in a crisis.

He is more inspired who wakes up early though in a crisis, takes a bath and prepares himself than he who stays in bed watching television. Taking action does not need to be complicated. Simple action points like keeping your house in order, washing your clothes, engaging in conversations and so on can help in a major way before the major break comes.

> *"In order to succeed in your assignment, learn how to create a 24-Hour Masterpiece every day"*
> —Dr. Mike Murdock

## 11. Identify Opportunities:

I am talking about immediate opportunities here. The biggest reason as to why we do not see opportunities is our conditioned thinking. Let me bring this into perspective. Ben was an executive. When he lost his job, he thought that the only place he could get another opportunity was as an executive. His wife thought the same way as well as his friends and parents.

The problem is that this kind of thinking limits us greatly. For example, there are times when Ben did not have two coins to rub together, let alone feed his wife and child. He was waiting for a major breakthrough. In the housing estate where Ben stayed, he had about 10 neighbors who owned vehicles. They would take their vehicles for washing occasionally and pay for it. Was that an immediate opportunity for Ben? Of course it was!

Did he see it? Nope. I think another major reason as to why we do not see opportunities is our penchant to peddle our status around. We do not want to 'lower ourselves'. I think the greatest test of maturity in terms of our resilience index is first, the knowledge that the setback is temporary. Secondly, it is our ability to overlook our so-called status and 'stoop low' to take up something that is of a 'lesser class' than we have already attributed to ourselves.

Do this in humility with the knowledge that the setback will come to pass. In fact, there is so much to learn when you willfully decide to operate at a level lower than your class. I am ready to bet that no degree can equal your graduation from the school of humility. Indeed, in humility there are great opportunities.

The following are where you could look to unearth opportunities:

1. From a class or classes lower than what you have now
2. From your Personal Brand exercises
3. From your SWOT analysis
4. From a deliberate and relentless 'hunt' of opportunities
5. From ideas that come to you as you take action in other areas

Identifying opportunities unearths your entrepreneurial side that all along you thought you did not have. If this can be a constant habit in your life, I can predict that in ten years from this setback, you would be a world changer.

> *"Life has three basic pleasures: Creativity, progress and completion"*
> ~Dr. Mike Murdock.

**12. Use your tongue as a weapon:**
You will find the following words in the next chapter, quoting Ben: "I know one thing: I am a world changer. I do not know how and when that would happen, but one thing I know is that I am meant to be a world changer. My life is meant to count, to touch others positively. That I am sure"

It is very easy to be positive when all is going well. However, the greatest need for us to be positive and hopeful is when we are experiencing a crisis or facing a setback. Amazingly, the greatest weapon we have at all times in our lives is right under our nose!

Obviously, at the time of a setback, there seems to be a negative aura going around your environment. If you are not careful, there could also be a defeatist attitude that creeps in. Your greatest weapon against these things is not a sudden change in your fortunes. Your greatest weapon is your resilient words that you speak even as the setback pervades.

There is tremendous power that can be created with the words that you choose to speak. I am so amazed how feelings can change in less than an hour through words. In order to navigate your setback, you need to write down positive, hopeful, future-oriented recitals. The following is how you can use your tongue as a weapon:

a) Write down an inspiring short sentence about your life
b) Select a place where you can say that sentence to yourself real loud
c) Select a time (or times) that you can recite that sentence
d) At one take, recite your sentence over and over and over again, at least fifteen minutes.
e) Do this daily and religiously without breaking the cycle.

Jesus Christ said that what comes out of a person is what defiles him, not what goes in. This means that the *effect* of what has been going in has the capacity to defile you. You need to be in direct charge of what goes into your mind.

Reciting these positive things about you like you would take a dosage of medicine to cure a disease is critical. It creates a sense of hope and firmly re-calibrates your mind from an otherwise negative perspective that is rendered by most setbacks.

A good example that I use is this: "Every day, I am living a life full of Divine energy and vitality, generating a heavy dose of powerful inspiration, impacting this world with a message of hope, wellness and abundance".

I also paraphrase a scripture in the Bible from The Message translation. It goes something like this: "God has promised that He will bless me with everything He has, bless and bless and bless. Therefore, in blessing I am blessed and in multiplication, I am multiplied".

This is powerful stuff. You can find out more about using your tongue from http://life-signatures.com While there, search for two articles titled: "The greatest speech ever", and "Why You Need to Hire Yourself as Your Own Prophet".

## 13. Take Charge of Your Environment:
One little thing, although tremendously powerful is taking care of your immediate environment and surroundings in that there are no seeds of doom and gloom around. What we see and hear have a great impact on our feelings.

Moreover, you will get tremendous positive feedback around you if you instituted some form of order. If you were in a crisis, it is important that not everything in your life is in disarray. There should not be loads of utensils in the dishwasher going unwashed for days. The house should not be dirty. Your clothes should not go unwashed for days. Things should not be thrown all over the place creating chaos.

When you sort out this immediate aspect of your life, inherently, you start building loads of hope. I guarantee you that as you begin to 'clean house' you will start feeling a surge of energy rising. Somehow, an aura of hope and energy is released around an organized environment.

On the contrary, there is lots of heaviness that you would feel around a chaotic environment. In fact, a disorganized environment tends to cement the illusion that your crisis is the worst ever and that you have nothing to do about it. You know this is true.

Most importantly, you should be extremely proactive about the inspiration that you create from your environment. If you are in a crisis, it is not good spending the whole day constantly watching negative news.

Dr. Mike Murdock says that you should schedule your joys because your troubles will schedule themselves. I agree. I think you need to schedule exactly what you will watch, what you will read, what you will listen to and what discussions you will engage yourself in. In our day and age, we have loads of information that is instructive, inspirational and motivational.

If you are going through a crisis and are not proactively deciding the input in your environment, you are doing a disservice to yourself. The present world is also full of negatives that are happening daily: murders, rapes, robberies, scams, natural disasters and many others. One hour of exposure to these kinds of input overwhelms your heart with heaviness.

Ithat is said that for every negative thing said or thought, you will need a counter response in the positive at least 14 times to neutralize its effect. One more input will then reinforce the positive. It is therefore instructive that we take charge of our environment, ridding it of every negative innuendos if need be.

Taking charge of your environment puts you in control of a very critical aspect of your mind: your state. Your mental state determines your daily output. You want to come out stronger and wiser from a crisis? Manage the environment that controls your mental state.

**14. Identify available resources:**
I heard Dr. Cindy Trimm one day say the following powerful statement about empowerment:

*"Empowerment is a process through which an individual or a group of individuals are assisted, equipped and strengthened in order to discover their potential, identify their capabilities and to access available resources while at the same time enabling them to exploit and leverage opportunities in order for them to maximize their strengths and their potentials as they hone their skills and abilities"*

What a loaded statement this is! I know she is talking about being empowered yet I am championing empowering yourself! There are so many nuggets that we can learn from Dr. Cindy Trimm's message on empowerment. That message oozes lots of options.

- She talks of potential…everyone including the day old baby today have this. We have discussed this already.
- She talks of capability…we all have this no matter what state we are in. It comes in different measures. We have already discussed this under Personal Branding.

- She talks of opportunities…these are the wild card of options.
- She talks of maximizing strengths, skills and abilities…these can be done with little or no money.
- She talks of available resources…there are so many here that we are literally blind to during hardship.

I bet that the most important question to ask here is: How do I identify the available resources? This is a major turning point during the crisis. Up until now, most of the options we have talked about have involved looking at your 'acres of diamonds'.

We have gone through an extensive introspection to unearth your 'value add' in life as well as to focus on your daily behavior. I must say however that an internal focus alone is not enough to take you out of the crisis. It is indeed the beginning point which many people ignore. For the most part, people start looking for help without offering any help in return.

We usually equate lack of resources with lack of funds. The Bible says that 'money is the answer to everything'.

In order to identify the available resources:

a) **Identify your audience:** a person or people you can serve with your brand
b) **Identify what value you can add:** what problem can you solve for them?
c) Clarify exactly how you intend to influence your audience with your value
d) **Determine in clear quantities** what resources you will need to accomplish this
e) **Determine exactly where you can find these resources,** starting from your immediate environment
f) **Consider offering your value 'pro-bono'** until you can start charging.
g) **Ask for help relentlessly** in obtaining these resources.

Notice that this is a lot different from the normal asking for help (which has its place). Normally, we ask for money to pay our rent, medical bills etc. Even if we do get the help, with time, people get tired of our needy situation.

While I was a member of the Rotary Club of Ntinda in Kampala, Uganda, I came across a boy who espoused this principle so well that I invited him as a guest speaker to our fellowship.

His dad is a peasant and has no ability to pay for his school fees. What this boy did was to form a small company that made artifacts out of pottery. He joined the Interacts Club, a teenage wing of the Rotary Club. With his artifacts, he told his story to his immediate audience and made sales that funded his education. I had seen very many people come to our fellowship as guest speakers and bored us with their lousy topics, but when that 16 year old boy took to the stand to talk, he offered value!

Ben did this initially when he started coaching people and it generated him some income. There is potential for growth here if it is the only thing you would be doing as you wait for your 'ship to come'. It might very well be the ship of your life.

## 15. Seek Help with pressing needs:
No man is an island. As I write this, I am in the Brong Ahafo region of Ghana. I was not able to go work because of a terrible flu that has kept me indoors. In the afternoon, a small boy came by my house and asked if he could get rid of the litter outside, mostly carton boxes. I did not understand his language. He spoke in broken English, mixing it with the local Twi dialect. I honestly thought that he was just interested in the carton boxes which I had no problem getting rid of. When I told him that I would go back to the house, he knelt down and spoke mixing his mother tongue and English.

> *"The reason welfare never works is because welfare was never meant to be permanent. It was meant to sustain you through a particular period of adversity so you could launch from that into a sustained period of blessing where you're not always waiting for someone to shake your hand. Because if you have to live off of people shaking your hand, you become a beggar in the kingdom, and you start manipulating people because you need them to shake your hand to make it. And that is not God's will*
> —T.D. Jakes, "Favor Aint Fair," Sermon, The Potter's House, Dallas, TX, July 2007

The only word that I grasped was 'school uniform'. I gathered that he must have been looking for money to pay for his school fees. Wow! What a way to ask. This boy dared indulge a total stranger who did not understand his language, waking him up from his bed rest so he could get help. I know that some people would say that maybe the boy was taking me for a ride, that he just wanted to fleece me. OK, what if he wasn't? And that is beside the point anyway.

The point is twofold:

  a) **We need help with pressing needs:** If you have not been building reserves before this crisis, chances are that you have some seriously pressing needs right now. Frankly, it is a bit cumbersome to do anything if the pressing needs of your current situation are not fulfilled. That is why we have friends and family. These two groups can be extremely instrumental in helping you out as you find your footing during the crisis.

However, we must know that pressing needs are not eternal needs. We should not take advantage of people by 'camping' in their houses during a crisis while at the same time we are doing nothing in an effort to bring respite to our condition.

In other words, the help you are seeking from people at this time is not permanent. Everyone has needs. If someone thinks that you will be relying on them perpetually for your supply, they might not want to get involved. In short, they are not God.

A better way of obtaining help has been discussed in the previous point.

b) **There are some people who want to help:** The boy who came by my house could as well have been me several years ago. It could be a loved one. I have gone through so much myself that it is easy to identify with those in need. Once in a while I do help out. The same applies to many people out there in life.

While Ben was serving at the radio station, his life had taken a serious beating. He had been evicted from his house with the landlord rightfully keeping his household goods (although it broke the landlord's heart to do this). As Ben kept offering value, one day a listener texted and told Ben of how appreciative she was to Ben's program and that Ben was a blessing. If Ben needed anything, he should not hesitate to ask.

Ben braved on for some weeks in hardship until he remembered his caller. He texted her and told her that this was now the time that he needed help. She was extremely instrumental in helping Ben move his family from a mosquito infested house in a rural location of town to a better housing unit as well as provide for his daily upkeep.

I also know that sometimes, it can be shameful to ask for help. I know of many people who could get help with their pressing need but cannot bring themselves to ask. On the same token, there are those who readily negate their responsibilities and rely solely on others with their pressing needs.

These are two extremes. There ought to be a balance, and this has been duly explained.

## 16. Volunteer:

You could either sit in your house all day and think of how bad life has turned out to be, or you could go out in the community and serve. There are many groups that you can be part of before a crisis. There are church groups as well as other social groups. Any time they have an activity going on, you should make your availability known.

I listened to Darlene Bishop share her story with Joni Lamb of how she lost her husband to a medical condition. Darlene said that one of the things that she did at that trying time of her life was to keep pouring herself out to others despite her loss.

There is tremendous value available when you in a crisis can serve others in their crisis. A subtle but powerful communication goes on in your brain saying that you are needed. This signal is not only sent to your brain, it is also sent to the people around you and to the 'universe' if you will. Somehow, your sense of usefulness attracts more activities in your life, the very thing that you need at this moment.

Am sure there are managers in the world that started out as volunteers. Chances are that they would not have gotten those positions if they had shrunk back because of adversity. The world responds favorably to the people who constantly display their usefulness in whatever format. The world responds in kind to people who shrink back while facing a crisis—it hides opportunities from them.

So you could go out and be counted today, or you could stay in your house holed up and rue your decisions that brought you to this state. A signal would be sent to your brain. It says that your usefulness is no more and ultimately, the world does not need you. The same message is also sent to the universe and the people around you.

This in turn has a devastating blow to your self esteem. It compounds your crisis and erodes your capacity. Just the fact that you will not be paid when you volunteer should not make you shrink back. In actual sense, there are great benefits when you do volunteer work.

a) You will meet people and form networks
b) You will have a chance to showcase your attitude
c) You will have an opportunity to learn new things
d) You will have an opportunity to show off your gifts and skills
e) You will get your mind off of your crisis which is a major blow to depression

f) You will probably get new ideas that you can work with
g) Chances are that you will learn about 'vacancies' available elsewhere.

**17. Learn to communicate who you really are:**
One of the most dreaded questions that you can ask someone in a crisis is this: "What do you do?" When Ben lost his job, he must have encountered that question countless times and fidgeted with every answer he gave back.

We live in a society that apportions our worth to what we do and not who we are. That is why people are so obsessed with titles than functions. In equal measure, most people who do not have titles tend to feel worthless.

Sometimes, a crisis normally gets rid of our titles. A divorce makes a married woman single, a retrenchment makes a worker jobless, death of a parent makes a child fatherless, loss of investments make an investor bankrupt, loss of a house makes a family homeless, and so on.

The 'new titles' that adversities give to us almost always espouse our ultimate fears. We need not accept these new titles. I am not saying that we are now living in denial. I am just saying that we choose to refuse to let a crisis define who we are, who we really are.

I think your definition is not based on the result of your setback. It is however the sum total of your deepest aspirations as well as your positive contribution to mankind. You should never forget that. Crucially important is the fact that there is a Designer behind the existence of every life. Your true identify and definition was crafted by the Designer even before the crisis hit you. The Designer obviously knew about the crises that you will face. He of course knew one thing: You are not what a crisis labels you to be; you are what he intended you to be. I think our greatest occupation on earth is to know what that intention is. It cost the Designer a reincarnation!

When you assume a victim title that has come as a result of a setback, you self-stigmatize yourself. You walk around unconsciously dispelling anything good that can be attracted to your life. You keep re-affirming what the world has dealt with you and not who you really desire to be.

---

*"We see the world not as it is, we see the world as we are"*
—Quote

---

We should understand that what we tell ourselves about ourselves is what we tell others about ourselves.

The world however never asks who you are. Check it out in your life. Have you ever been introduced by a friend or a colleague to someone new? What do they normally ask? They never ask who you are; they almost always ask 'what you do!' Can you remember the last time someone asked you who you are? Personally, I do not think I have ever been asked that question.

Yet, that is the most important question that you need to answer. As you give the answer, you need to do it with so much passion that the person you are communicating to would get it and would want to participate in whatever way.

When someone asks you what you do, tell them who you are. The fact of the matter is that who you are can never cease to be even when a crisis hits you.

Instead of dreading those moments when you have to introduce yourself or to answer that question, "what do you do?" you should look forward to providing an answer to your audience based on who you are. If you are careful enough, your breakthrough could come from this step alone.

For more information about how you can articulate who you really are, visit my page http://life-signatures.com

**18. Create a System:**
Do you wake up in the morning and there is nothing to do but watch television? It is because you do not have a system! Now, the word system sounds so technical and you might think that you need some classes to know how to install one.

In actual sense, you do know how to make a system. You have probably operated one before. A simple system is the study timetable you might have used either in primary school or in high school.

You need a system that your life can operate in on a daily basis. A good life has a rhythm of activities that create habits. These habits will build your character. The late Stephen R. Covey wrote a powerful book titled "The 7 Habits of Highly Effective people". This is nothing but a system. Those habits are not haphazard. They are carefully and intentionally selected and organized.

Any business worth its salt has systems. In fact, what the management does on a daily basis is to ensure that each part of the system is operating well, contributing to the overall well-being of the whole.

There is no better time to create your system than in the moment of a crisis.

This is one more step in not only generating your options but also organizing them.

Ideally, your system should be structured as follows:

a) **Internal system actions:** This part of your system is absolutely critical. With the analogy of a car, your internal system is the engine. Your internal system relates to feeding your mind, getting inspiration and staying motivated. It is a deliberate balance between being entertained and being educated. Conscious actions with the internal system include reading instructional and inspirational material, watching, listening and being involved in a mastermind group discussion.

b) **External system actions:** This part involves activities that you do on a daily basis. These activities stem from the exercises from the previous points. They could be activities that directly impact your wellbeing for now, or indirectly determine the long term direction of your life. As much as they are important, they come second to internal system actions.

Your goal is to organize a daily and weekly system that includes your action points that are non-negotiable.

Having a system gives you a sense of worth as well as a sense of direction, the very things that a life crisis impacts negatively upon. You will be eternally grateful that you took this step.

> *"You are not what a crisis labels you to be; you are what He intended you to be. I think our greatest occupation on earth is to know what that intention is. It cost the Designer a reincarnation"!*

## 19. Track Your Progress:

Having the system is one thing, working the system is quite another! Buying a self-help book is one thing, making sure that it is not 'shelf help' is another matter altogether. We need discipline in order to implement new habits in our lives. You will most definitely feel a sense of accomplishment once your system is in place. Chances are that that feeling might not last forever.

There are days that you will not feel like working the system at all. That is when your commitment will show. The best respite in those moments is to install a tracking mechanism for your system.

For example, do you know an estimated percentage level at which you really 'lived' in the past year? Well if you don't, chances are that you have only been existing and not really living.

A tracking mechanism helps you to record your actions on your non negotiable activities on a daily basis. We are not saying that everyday will be smooth sailing, but those days where you do not achieve what you set out to, you can record the reason. This helps you to analyze so as to make the needed adjustments to keep going.

The biggest advantage of a tracking system is that it helps you to stay consistent. The secret to your success is found not in what you do occasionally, but in what you do daily. Starting is easy. Keeping at it is the call of life.

A tracking mechanism will also help you to significantly reduce the 'inactivity gap'. This means that it will show you what aspect of your non negotiable activities has taken long to be implemented. There should be a very small gap between the continuity of an inspired action. In fact, the goal of your consistency is totally eliminate this gap.

If you want to be motivated, make this tracking mechanism a paramount thing daily. Studying your entries and reviewing your actions helps you get better and better. You even get smarter in operation; for example you realize that you can listen to something inspirational or read something instructional while travelling.

**20. Journal:**
During a setback, there are nuggets, principles, ideas and concepts that will come to your mind that would not have come in your 'normal' days. You need to have a 'global' view of these things as they happen. What I mean is that the lessons you are learning at this hour can help someone else.

I think the worst crisis we have in life in the modern day is mentorship. We have boys who have never been taught how to shave, how to be a gentleman, how to treat a lady, how to make investments and so on. Yet their predecessors faced lots of setbacks that certainly had lessons in them. We have young people who are going through heartbreaks and making lifetime vows as a result.

Nobody is mentoring them. Nobody is telling them that life can turn out better. A lady is heartbroken and she vows that all men are dogs. It becomes a self-fulfilling prophecy in that if she were to get into a relationship with another man, he turns out to be a dog.

Your setback or crisis today is not an isolated incident that should be written in your forgotten years of your life. Your setback is a vaccine, an antidote to someone else who has caught the same virus. It could very well be your children. History should not repeat itself.

When you learn these things while in your setback, take some time and write them down. Organize them well and think about them. Be ready to offer much needed advice to someone who needs it. Believe me, there are hundreds of people.

Chances are that you are now being molded as a messenger of hope, one who is able to comfort others who are going through the same setback or crisis. They will identify with you and you will most definitely identify with them. Journaling in your crisis is the fastest way of creating a remedy for someone else. Do not neglect it. Learn to review it.

Be sensitive to what comes out of your spirit…write it down and pursue it to its fullest. Chances are that as far as your true heart desires are concerned, your crisis can easily reveal it. This is because a crisis or a setback normally puts life in perspective more than comfort would. Do not hesitate to write down the dreams if they are revealed to you.

## 21. Where is God?
In the free E-Book download on the '21 Commandments to Mastermind your Comeback' ', I talk about the propensity of people seeking help from witchdoctors, fortune tellers, and other 'dark forces'.

Throughout this book, little reference has been made on the role of God Almighty in our crisis. In fact in Chapter four, I have controversially discounted the option of 'waiting on God' as your main and only strategy to use while waiting for your 'breakthrough'.

In talking about God last, I am intentionally showing you that much as God is our Helper in time of trouble, He seldom performs miracles to immediately yank us out of our setbacks. Even when He does, he will greatly count on our input and our availability. In other words, we must do something to play our part in bringing about the miracle. That is what this book is all about. If God's existence was to solely help us out of our setbacks on day two, then he would never have said the following:

*"All things work together for good for those who love the Lord and are called according to his purpose"* –Romans 8: 28

I am therefore in no way saying that you should seek God last in the times of trouble. I am saying that you should not limit God by your inactivity dubbed 'waiting on God'. God anticipates us to go through challenges so we can be victorious. Jesus Christ said, "In this world, you will face very many tribulations, but be of good cheer, I have overcome the world."

I was intrigued the other day as I studied God's Word in the Book of Revelation. God Almighty has different messages to different people in different places. Most of these people had one setback or another. Do you know what God said to them? For each and every one of them, God said in essence, "I know your setbacks"

He would then proceed rebuke them and carefully show them what they ought to do to orchestrate a comeback! God is interested in your comeback and has instructions for you to do the same!

Then, God would crown his message by promising a reward. Each and every one of the seven churches had a promise that is structured in this format: "He who overcomes, I will…" and then the said promise is stated. Each one had a different promise, just as each one had a different message, and a different setback.

As you can see, God required people to do something. Believing God is one thing. Praying to God is another. They have their places that must never be under-estimated. However, doing nothing on our part in the process of waiting for a miracle is simply unwise.

I must strongly indicate here that the option of prayer is more powerful than a nuclear bomb. Stating this concept last does not mean that prayer should be an afterthought. Prayer alone during a setback gives a lot of help to you:

- Prayer helps to unburden yourself
- Prayer helps to commit your 'impossibilities' to an all powerful God
- Prayer made rightly helps you to win the battle over your damaged emotions
- Prayer in the Spirit helps to uncover ideas that you could implement for the day
- Prayer during a crisis deepens your spiritual muscle like no other time
- Prayer will help grow a deep intimacy with God especially at this time

Prayer is a must yet this book admonishes us that it is not the only option. There are some other actions that can be taken *alongside* praying. Taking other actions does not mean that you are of little faith in that you cannot wait for God to work His miracles for you. It does not mean that you are 'trying to help God like Abraham did'. It just means that you are offering to God what you have as a seed for your harvest.

Granted, I must admit that any action that you take towards orchestrating your comeback must be God-centered. You cannot steal your way out of poverty. You cannot rob some people to become wealthy. In the same token, you cannot involve other 'powers' that are not of God in helping you out.

A major trap that people fall into is seeking 'supernatural powers' to either assist them out of trouble or keep the trouble away. God's supernatural powers were never intended to be used pre-dominantly to solve our crises while at the same time negating our available options.

But make no mistake about it; God's supernatural power is real. People in adverse situations have experienced it. God does answer prayers and has invited us to pray to Him expecting answers. It is not my mandate to discuss this facet at length. Indeed, there are hundreds of books that cover that topic pretty well.

My mandate in this book is to open our eyes so that we can realize that we are not helpless when we have setbacks. We should realize that we have myriads of options available which God can multiply the results as we use them. Your responsibility towards God in your crisis is as follows:

a) Seek continually to know Him. Jeremiah 29:13; Romans 10:13
b) Seek to know His purpose for your life. Jeremiah 29:11
c) Remain obedient to His Word
d) Serve Him with all your heart. Mark 12:30
e) Serve others with what you have. Mark 12:31

So there you have it. In actual sense, all these things need to be done not just to help us through a crisis. These things ought to be done in order that we can lead fruitful lives in whatever phase of the cycle we find ourselves in and also on a daily basis. These 21 points have been written with the focus of empowering people at various levels of life to become better and more purposeful. You do not need to be in a crisis to read and use these principles. They can help you greatly even when you are out of a crisis.

These principles are not in any way to be used and dumped. These are to become part and parcel of our daily living. You might not need all the 21. You might just need the right combination to unlock your life.

Be sure to obtain the corresponding workbook from http://life-signatures.com that has exercises and pointers you can use as you mastermind your comeback.

I believe you are in this world at these exciting moments for a good reason. You have survived many things so far and are not dead. There is a good reason. For now, let me say these words, "There is hope."

# CHAPTER 10:
## There is Hope!

As we wrap up, it is important for us to talk once more about hope. It is important to think about chance. It pays for us to consider opportunities, but most certainly, it is critical for us to understand destiny. There was this time that young Ben was in college. He was one of the happiest lads around. In fact, very many students hustled just to sit next to Ben during the lectures. He was a ball of energy. He radiated hope, intelligence, humor, care and dedication.

As the days came and went, the dark clouds of despair started hanging around him. He knew one way or another that it would happen. He was afraid of it. Eventually, the despair started to show. Sadness gripped his face. The exuberance was replaced by silence. The laughter was gone. The joy he radiated was suffocated by fear and this stark reality of what would happen to him.

Ben had come back to the city under the auspices of a generous family friend who took him in like one of his own. He was a parishioner in the church that Ben's dad had overseen before being ruthlessly transferred. Ben was to stay with this family just long enough to graduate. That time had come…and Ben knew that he would have no option but to retreat to the village.

Over the months in college, Ben had befriended a lady who was newly Christian. She noticed his despondency and just wanted to be there for him. After a joint prayer session in the squash court at college, Ben had a heart to heart with Jackie. What Ben told Jackie that day is the crux of this chapter as we finish his story.

You see, Ben did not know at that time that one day he would live in a foreign country. He did not know at that moment while talking to Jackie that his wife would be from a different country. Ben had no idea that he would impact thousands through 'The Hour of prayer'. He did not know that one day he would be interviewed on radio and TV stations. Yet that chilly morning, Ben said these words to Jackie:

*"I know one thing: I am a world changer. I do not know how and when that would happen, but one thing I know is that I am meant to be a world changer. My life is meant to count, to touch others positively. That I am sure"*

Ben remembers that that was one of the driest statements he had ever made. He did not feel any unction about it. He was too plagued with the adversity that was coming his way. Yet he spoke those words. Ben reckoned that he had come through so much.

Up until that time, he had walked barefoot for a decade and a half, had been hospitalized as a kid but came out, had lost his first born brother while enduring a rather challenging childhood. He had desired to join University and earn a degree, such a hungry lad for knowledge, but that was not forthcoming due to this and that. Yet Ben knew that he was meant for better things.

It would be very imprudent not to talk about the Biblical Job while talking about adversity and hope. We know from the scriptures that this man endured so much adversity that it took three days of silence to try figure it out in a conversation with his friends. This man's story was always Ben's favorite in moments of adversity. In moments when his heart was gripped with fear, Ben found comfort in knowing that another soul did go through worse.

From the story of Job, Ben found out that this man asked God, his friends, and the world, deep seated questions. Maybe you have asked yourself the same questions as Job did at one time in your life:

- Job 3:11 Why did I not die at birth, come out from the womb and expire?
- Job 3:12 Why did the knees receive me? Or why the breasts, that I should nurse?
- Job 3:16 Or why was I not as a hidden stillborn child, as infants who never see the light?
- Job 3:20 Why is light given to him who is in misery, and life to the bitter in soul?
- Job 3:23 Why is light given to a man whose way is hidden, whom God has hedged in?

Ben remembers that sometimes he would be so afraid that he longed for the night just to close his eyes and forget about his troubles. Then of course the morning would come. His stomach would tighten like a knot as the fear pervaded. We cannot even begin to imagine the psychological hardship that this soul was going through. After the season of asking questions like Job did, there follows a season of silence. At this moment, talk is cheap. All the questions have been asked. No answer has been forthcoming. So why bother ask any more? And that sometimes is the tragedy…when we stop asking questions.

The truth of the matter however is that there is answers to each of these valid questions. The interesting thing is that each of these questions has the same answer. Do you know it?

To be entirely honest, we all need to ask these Job-like questions as often as possible. Interestingly enough, Ben used to do exactly that but not from a heart of adversity, but from a spirit of longing. There was this time that he had to go back and stay with his younger brother and cousin at his elder brother's house. You see, Ben was not able to pay his bills anymore and needed help. He fought that move so hard until he perceived that his family was tired of his stubbornness. He gave in.

As his routine, early in the morning, Ben would be up praying…and asking God those questions. Ben remembers that his cousin was so touched by this kind of passionate praying that he said that his prayer life had been impacted, and that he would never be the same again!

Why are you here? Why have you been preserved all this time? Why didn't that sickness take you out? Why hasn't the adversity killed you? What are you doing here? Why are you reading these words? Do you realize that you are still here? There is only one answer to all these questions. That answer is the same to all the questions that Brother Job asked. Do you know it?

We cannot rule out hardship from our fleeting lives. We might spend half our lives protecting ourselves from adversity, but that would be folly. One way or another, it would show up. The greatest adversity however is when we do not know that single answer to these deep seated questions! It is a dark day when a soul does not have the general overview of life that the answer to these questions provides. It makes the adversity even darker, heavier and at the worst, useless. It resonates with what the teacher said, "Meaningless, meaningless, utterly meaningless, everything is meaningless!"

What a mean word, 'meaningless'! It is meaningless to have a business that does not profit.

It is meaningless to spend all on the pleasures that our souls long for and be dissatisfied still!

It really is meaningless to have lived and never mattered to anyone!

It is meaningless to toil one's entire life and go to the grave just having preserved your life through the years!

And ultimately, it is meaningless to have or live a life with no purpose!

Your life, my friend is the most valuable asset under the sun. Your life has a purpose. The question is: Do you know it? Do you know that your life has a definite purpose? That would be the first revelation, the general one. This is exactly what Ben was telling Jackie back in college. He was saying in essence that "I know that I am not myself lately. I know I look sad and despondent, but I also know that somehow, my life has a meaning. I do not know what that meaning is. I do not have a grip of it as yet. But I just do know that my life was meant to count. My life has some form of significant meaning"

And that, ladies and gentlemen, is the answer to all of Job's questions.

- "Why did I not die at birth, come out from the womb and expire"? Because your life has a meaning, Brother Job.
- "Why did the knees receive me? Or why the breasts, that I should nurse?" Because your life has a purpose, Brother Job.
- "Or why was I not as a hidden stillborn child, as infants who never see the light?" Because your life has a significance, Brother Job.
- "Why is light given to him who is in misery, and life to the bitter in soul..." Because they are needed and their lives are important to the world, Brother Job.
- "Why is light given to a man whose way is hidden, whom God has hedged in?" Because they too have a purpose, Brother Job.

Why are you here? Why have you been *preserved* through all the trouble, hardship and adversity that have come your way so far? I will tell you why. You have been preserved for greater good. Your life is meant to count. Your life is meant to be fruitful and to be a blessing to one other person. You are needed on earth, otherwise you would be dead! You were born to have a meaning on earth; otherwise you would never have been conceived, let alone born!

You see, even though it was hazy in his eyes, Ben knew that he had a purpose to serve this world. He was convinced and convicted that his purpose was older than him, because it was created first. I totally agree with him. Everyone has this meaning in their lives, including the madman in the streets today. Some people have it so clear in their mind what it really is…for others, it is a simple spark that keeps flickering away in their souls.

There was this time that Ben was alone in the house while his dad was still a minister in the big city. He was watching Christian television, one program after another, soaking his spirit and making it pliable. A preacher came on and talked about 'great men'. He said that the greatest thing on earth would be to be committed and faithful with whatever it is that you have been given. He inspired Ben so much. Then, as the preacher came to a closing of his message he made a call.

He said that if there was anyone in the auditorium or anybody watching would consider the call, they should stand and be counted. Ben remembers that with tears in his eyes, he did stand up. A young boy just into his twentieth year, he stood to be counted. Unlike when he spoke to Jackie his friend back in college, this time round it were just him and his God. God knows Ben's heart was true that day. God knows that Ben had not been swayed by the persuasion of the preacher. God knows that Ben felt it deep inside his heart even before the preacher mentioned. To this day, Ben has not forgotten the commitment he made to God… because Ben knew that his life has a purpose.

Believe me, there is such a thing as a spark in everyone's soul. I feel it deep inside my sanctified gut that nobody comes empty. I dare say that everyone was intended for the better of others. After all, that is what a life of purpose is all about.

At the expense of sounding annoyingly repetitive and 'copy catty', Myles Munroe has said that the richest places in the world are graveyards. From that concept…do you know the greatest regret the world over? Do you know when this regret happens? Let me tell you. The greatest regret that is faced worldwide is when a soul is at its deathbed. You know that the curtain is pulling down on you. For some reason you just know. Yet you also know that the greatest omission of your entire life is not being faithful to the spark. This comes with such finality that is basically unfathomable.

The above scenario is both good news and bad news. Why bad news? Well, there is nothing you can do about the spark on your deathbed. The spark was meant to be fanned in the initial and prime years of your life. Such a sorry state of helplessness. Such a heavy sense of wasted years even though your life was filled with all the activities, all the motions. Such a heavy sense of regret. Friend, that is the hard knuckled bad news for you. Do you like it? Are you ready for it? You see, It is always forthcoming, unless…

Now, how about some good news? Are you ready? Anyone reading this today has that proverbial second chance. Well, unless of course you are some kind of dead phantom moving around in cyberspace. My point is here is twofold.

First, you are still alive… and therefore you and I have that opportunity to be faithful to the spark. Secondly, the spark is not just that. It is an extremely powerful force that I dare say is older than you. Your spark was there before you were created. In fact, you were created centered around that spark. It is so awesome a power that no amount of heartache, rejection, sin, tribulations, embarrassment, lack, hardship and anything negative from whatever place you can think of can turn it off! It has been rained on by myriads of the good and bad… but friend, the spark still lives on!

Your calling and mine my friend is to be ever faithful to that spark. One thing is for sure here… nobody else can fan your spark to a mighty fire. You know why? Well, because they have their own sparks to fan! On the same token, you cannot fan somebody else's spark... you've got your own! Everyone born is called to have a Life Signature, and that calling is to be faithful to the smallest embers of fire that lie within us. This and this alone is one of the most precious treasures in the world... much more precious than the oil that they have just discovered in East Africa. You think nuclear is powerful? Wait until your spark is fanned into a mighty fire!

You see, a wavering spirit is the enemy of success, whose first born is failure. Much as it is OK to try this and that (sometimes we really cannot realize the spark at the first go), eventually we must settle down in life to what really matters. What really matters might not be what the 'system' has said. It might not be what our parents, guardians and teachers have indicated. For the most part, what matters in life is that one thing, that authentic spark that has been flickering in the distant benign of our very core. That spark, ladies and gentlemen is the reason as to why we are alive today. It is our true passion, our true calling... and we are not greater than it. We need to be true to it, and fan it aflame.

We already mentioned earlier that life has two facets: What we have control over, and what you have no control over. Ours is to stop worrying on what is happening in the dimensions beyond our control and focus our energies on fanning our spark. At times it seems boring, tiring and frustrating, but we have got to remain faithful. And of course there is that small matter of 'life not making sense at all' even as we fan our sparks. Today, you might be in a painful or even an embarrassing life situation. Make sure that that small 'punctuation' does not define your view of life. Instead, let that punctuation make your life appear human, and believable. If you look at the life through the glasses of the 'punctuations', you risk neglecting the vision and belittling the spark.

Today you could be stuck in an embarrassing moment; tomorrow you could be dining with CEOs and first ladies. That is Life. Being faithful to the spark is by a large margin also a function of our mentality. This means that in the wake of the 'punctuations', your mental accent and an affirmation is that 'all is well...all will be well, and in the end, I will not regret'.

We started by saying that adversity is common to man. We end by stating that what you are facing today cannot kill you, it will instead make you stronger. We are here to tell you that there is beauty out of ashes, there is strength out of fear, there is gladness out of mourning, and there is peace out of despair.

What you are facing today is one of the most temporary things you will ever face. It is not here to stay. It has come yes, but just the same way it came your way, it will go! You see, this is the hope that should encourage you to action. There is hope that you are a victor.

You most definitely will come out better,
You will come out stronger,
You will come out more committed,
You will come out more sensitive and caring.
You will not die because of disaster and adversity,
You will instead be a deliverer of many who will face the same or worse.

You need not give up,
You are in need of holding on one more minute, one more day.
It might take a phone call,
It might take one visit,
It might take one email,
It might be one effort that you did,

In its time, your breakthrough will come. Your dream will become a reality. Although it delays, wait for it. At the moment, the dream might seem long gone and even dead. But then again, we already said that that is an illusion. It is not the reality.

The subject of dreams and visions remains extremely fascinating. It is through dreams and visions that everything we see finds substance. As such, there is always a life cycle of a dream. Dreams always speak. Dreams are always babies needing to be nurtured.

Dreams have a conception. Every dream longs to be fulfilled. The very reason as to why the dream appears to you and I is that we have been found worthy to gestate it! I write this because very many people, sometimes including myself get so discouraged at the conception of a dream, especially during a crisis in life.

*This vision-message is a witness pointing to what's coming. It aches for the coming--it can hardly wait! And it doesn't lie. If it seems slow in coming, wait. It's on its way. It will come right on time—Habakkuk 2:3(The Message Bible)*

They see nothing but impossibilities whenever a dream has found them worthy. In fact to some people the recipe of misery is an overwhelming dream. However, a great visionary realizes one very crucial aspect about dreams and visions. You are not the only activator in the picture.

There is always the unseen that is behind the concept of the dream. Needless to say, there comes a time where (seemingly) someone's dream dies. Paradoxically, this ought to be really good news. Why? Because you recognized the dream, and in your hand it (seemingly) died.

If you never recognized the dream, that is if you never conceived it, then you would never have recognized its 'death'. Dreams die because the carrier or 'gestator' if you will has come to their wits end. In fact, the dream carrier is so bogged down with their own survival that they have no strength to activate their dreams. All they do is wish, long, desire…and sometimes…pray.

Any dream that has died on you is worth pursuing. It's worth re-activating. It's worth taking a second look. It's worth looking at from a different dimension for its re-activation. I dare say that sometimes, all it needs is for the carrier to 'surrender'. Recognize that it's not just you in the picture as far as that dream is concerned.

Give way to the other players although invisible in the dream to help you. You might need a little wisdom. You might need a little counsel. You might need your eyes to be opened a little. You might need to see the excitement of someone who hears about your dream, although now considered dead. You might need a little prayer.

Sometimes the death of a dream is really the beginning of its unparalleled resurrection and realization.

Let me share this powerful story that I heard when I attended the Visionary Business University class 2010 organized by Jeffrey Howard. It is given by Marcia Weider, the CEO of Dream University and faculty member of Visionary Business University 2010 in her interview with Jeffrey Howard. Let me say this: Don't you ever give up on that dream. Hold fast to it. Do not worry about the copy cats…as long as it means something to your heart…it shall come to pass. The ultimate death of a dream is when you no longer carry it… that's when it dies never to be resurrected.

# EPILOGUE

## THE STORY OF MACIA WEIDER

So the people that inspire me the most are the everyday people. My favorite story - and I guess it's become the signature story because I tell it so much --but it's a brief story and I really love this. I was giving a talk in Portland, Oregon and a young man came up to me and he said, "Thank you for your talk today, it really inspired me, I'm a long way from home." And I looked at him – he was very tall, very unusual, very dark skin, almost blue. And I knew he was from far, far away. He had said "I'm a long way from home." And I said, "Oh, I travel a lot too." And he said, "Well, this might be a little different you see this is the first Sunday of my life that I've been away from my tribe." Of course I stopped what I was doing, "Your tribe? Who are you? Where are you from?" And he said, "I'm from Kenya, Africa. I'm part of the Maasai Warrior Tribe." And I said, "Well, what are you doing in Portland? (laugh)

He said, "When I was very young, very, very young, I became ill and my mother took me to a near-by medical clinic. And from that day forward my dream was to become a doctor, but it was impossible. There was no training, available, and you didn't leave the tribe," he said. It just wasn't done." He said.

"As I grew up. I shared the dream with everyone and everyone including my own family told me to forget it. They told me it was a fantasy. They'd roll their eyes and told me to go back to work."

He said, "But I never forgot it, and recently around my 18th birthday, a visitor came from your country and it turned out that he was a writer for the Washington Post. He wrote my story. A few weeks later, a couple in Portland, OR happened to read it.

I was invited to apply for undergraduate work. And in a matter of months I was accepted at the University of Portland." And I looked at him and said, "It must have been the happiest day of your life." He said, "No, it was the worst day. It was horrific." My family didn't have the resources to send me off to America to follow a dream of becoming a doctor. It just really was impossible." And he literally said Jeff, he said, "I did the only thing I knew to do. I prayed for a miracle, and that's what I got.

Four families came forward. Each one made the commitment one year apiece to feed me, to house me, to buy my books, to basically love me and be my family while I was so far from home." Well, he's telling the story, and I am a puddle, as you are right now. We just turned into puddles, because it's just unbelievable. And what he said next is what really makes him one of the great visionaries that I ever met. He said, "But it wasn't until today when I heard you speak so passionately about dreams, that I really got clear about what I need to do. I need to become a doctor, of course, that's my dream. But then I need to go home. I need to go back to my tribe and be an example that no dream is impossible, and the extraordinary things that can happen when we gather together as a tribe or as a team."

I just hear that story and I think: No dream is impossible. And I don't care how big your obstacles are, or how little you have, or what the issues are - if you really are committed to your dream. Then I would say, "Put a stake in the ground. Set an intention. Put yourself in right relationship to it with your integrity, because in my work: intention and integrity together form the core building block for making your dreams come true. So it's not enough to say you want it, you have to do something about it. And when I watch people do that, miracles do occur.

One way or another, your season of adversity will come and it will go, just like it did for Ben. As we close his story, it is prudent to learn that he actually is the one who has been writing all along, narrating his own story.

Our once stuck executive is now an author of hope. Without the adversity, he might not have been able to write all these.

For those of you whose situations are so dire that like Job you have sat for days in silence, there is hope. In all literature written since time immemorial, there is one Man who declared that His entire *purpose* on earth is to help you. He spoke the following immortal words, the words that fill us with hope all the time. As we close this chapter and this book, let us be reminded of these words:

*The Spirit of GOD, the Master, is on me because GOD anointed me. He sent me to preach good news to the poor, heal the heartbroken, Announce freedom to all captives, pardon all prisoners.*

*GOD sent me to announce the year of his grace-- a celebration of God's destruction of our enemies-- and to comfort all who mourn,*

*To care for the needs of all who mourn in Zion, give them bouquets of roses instead of ashes, Messages of joy instead of news of doom, a praising heart instead of a languid spirit. Rename them "Oaks of Righteousness" planted by GOD to display his glory.*

*They'll rebuild the old ruins, raise a new city out of the wreckage. They'll start over on the ruined cities, take the rubble left behind and make it new.*

*You'll hire outsiders to herd your flocks and foreigners to work your fields, But you'll have the title "Priests of GOD," honored as ministers of our God. You'll feast on the bounty of nations, you'll bask in their glory.*

*Because you got a double dose of trouble and more than your share of contempt, Your inheritance in the land will be doubled and your joy go on forever.*

*"Because I, GOD, love fair dealing and hate thievery and crime, I'll pay your wages on time and in full, and establish my eternal covenant with you.*

*Your descendants will become well-known all over. Your children in foreign countries Will be recognized at once as the people I have blessed."*

*I will sing for joy in GOD, explode in praise from deep in my soul! He dressed me up in a suit of salvation, he outfitted me in a robe of righteousness, As a bridegroom who puts on a tuxedo and a bride a jeweled tiara.*

*For as the earth bursts with spring wildflowers, and as a garden cascades with blossoms, so the Master, GOD, brings righteousness into full bloom and puts praise on display before the nations.*

—Jesus Christ (Isaiah 61)

Printed in Great Britain
by Amazon